Eve's Pilgrimage

TINA BEATTIE

Eve's Pilgrimage

A WOMAN'S QUEST FOR THE CITY OF GOD

BURNS & OATES
A Continuum imprint
LONDON • NEW YORK

BURNS & OATES
A Continuum imprint
The Tower Building, 11 York Road, London SE1 7NX
370 Lexington Avenue, New York, NY 10017-6503
www.continuumbooks.com

ISBN 0 8601 2323 5

Typeset by CentraServe Ltd, Saffron Walden, Essex
Printed and bound in Great Britain by
Biddles Ltd, Guildford and King's Lynn

Acknowledgements:
Veronica Zundel, 'Deception', used by permission from
Faith in Her Words, Six Centuries of Women's Poetry,
compiled by Veronica Zundel (Lion, 1991); Svetlana
Alexievich, *Voices from Chernobyl*, extracts used by
permission from Aurum Press, London; 'In Bread we
bring you, Lord', © Copyright Kevin Mayhew Ltd.,
Buxhall, Stowmarket, Suffolk IP14 3BW, extract used by
permission from *Hymns Old & New*.

Every effort has been made to locate holders of
copyright material. However, the author and publishers
would be interested to hear from any copyright holders
not credited herein so that full acknowledgement may
be made in future editions.

Contents

List of Illustrations

Preface

This book was finished before the attack on the World Trade Center and the Pentagon. I am writing this Preface in the immediate aftermath when the world seems to stand on the edge of an abyss. The last chapter in particular now haunts and disturbs me. I did not plan that chapter, and I am not sure why it took the shape it did. I offer it as an elegy and a prayer for the city – that great symbol that encompasses the vision and the folly, the solidarity and the violence, of our shared humanity. Ultimately, the city is a work of redemption, wherein we transform the garden of creation into the history and the culture of our human becoming. In the turmoil of our broken and frightened lives, may the city be for us a symbol of that eternal city, the New Jerusalem, where one day, peoples and faiths will come together to live forever in the justice and mercy of God – Yahweh, Allah, Trinity.

> There are questions we are the solution
> to, others whose echoes we must expand
> to contain. Circular as our way
> is, it leads not back to that snake-haunted
> garden, but onward to the tall city
> of glass that is the laboratory of the spirit.
>
> R. S. Thomas, 'Emerging'

For Dave

'He has taken me to his banquet hall,
and the banner he raises over me is love.'

Introduction

In August 2000 I was invited to Rome to give a presentation at a Pontifical Marian Conference, as part of the Jubilee celebrations. Those who negotiated my invitation implied that they wanted a feminist perspective on Mary, but I found my feminist sensibilities frozen by the prospect of standing up in front of some of the church's most celebrated and conservative Mariologists. In the event I gave what was probably the worst paper of my academic career to date. But that trip to Rome was a pilgrimage of momentous significance for me. It marked a point in my life when I found myself taking stock of the distance I had travelled symbolically, spiritually and physically, since I became a Roman Catholic while living in Zimbabwe in 1987, as a married woman and mother of four little children. In the intervening years, I had come to live in Bristol with my family, taken a degree in theology and religious studies, completed a doctorate on Marian theology and symbolism, and embarked on an unexpected career at the age of forty as a writer and lecturer in theology. I had also discovered feminism – at least twenty years later than most of my contemporaries. My experiences of love and marriage, sexuality and motherhood, the making and breaking of relationships, the treasuring of friendships, all had to find a space of accommodation and meaning within these two new and improbable convictions which had found a space of tempestuous cohabitation within me – Catholicism and feminism.

A pilgrimage is what the anthropologist Victor Turner refers to as a liminal experience.[1] It is a time of risk and transformation, when a person's identity and social role are briefly suspended as he or she experiences a stage of transition or a rite of passage. I did not intend my trip to Rome to be a pilgrimage, but in retrospect that is what it became. I had recently completed my doctoral studies and I did not yet know what direction the future might take, so I had a sense of being open to new beginnings. I had for the first time left my family for longer than a few days, so it represented a realization that the years of being bound physically and emotionally to my children's dependencies were coming to an end. I was emerging from a painful time of personal crisis, so I was in that heightened state of vulnerability and hope when one must learn to love again and love differently. After 25 years of marriage I was discovering for the first time the enormity, the grief and the wonder of married love – something that I think few feminists have understood. And perhaps in an analogous way I was reassessing what it meant to be a Catholic, in that disturbing and enchanting city which symbolizes the best and the worst of the Catholic faith. Is my relationship with Catholicism capable of turning into a loving and committed marriage, or will it always be a turbulent love affair which might yet end in tears and a broken heart? I have no answer to that question, but it is one I continue to ask myself. Encoded within that question is another even more unanswerable one: what kind of faith and what kind of God does my Catholicism sustain?

That word 'God' has undergone intense scrutinies and trans-formations in the last 300 years of Western thought. In the late nineteenth century Friedrich Nietzsche declared that Western society, and in particular Christianity, had murdered God. God was dead. Since then, some philosophers and theologians have attempted to raise God, not this time as the real creative being who sustains but is infinitely other than the time and space of the material world, but as an empty symbol, a useful narrative device which helps us to tell a story about the world. Which God do I mean when I use that word? In what follows, is God in some sense 'real', someone I believe exists beyond anything human beings can say or imagine, or is 'God' a fiction without which this story and indeed every story might fall apart? To reflect on these questions would require a book in itself. Perhaps for me, God is the name of the void, of the sustaining absence at the heart of the world that is more acute and more real than the most vivid presence. g-O-d. The empty sphere at the centre, inadequately shaped by the ciphers of language, religion and culture, enigmatically encoded in nature as well as in human imagination. I am drawn again and again to Catherine of Siena's ravishment at the end of her life, when she cried in ecstasy or agony (who knows which, and can we really tell them apart?), 'You, eternal Trinity, are a deep sea: The more I enter you, the more I discover, and the more I discover, the more I seek you. You are insatiable, you in whose depths the soul is sated yet remains always hungry for you.'[2] Thérèse of Lisieux echoes Catherine when she writes, 'Love attracts love and mine soars up to You, eager to fill the abyss of Your love, but it is not even a drop of dew lost in the ocean.'[3] It is the God whom Catherine calls 'fire and abyss of love' that holds me, in Thérèse's words, 'an abyss whose depths I cannot plumb'. It is the Catholic Church that holds me back, gives shape to the abyss, and makes it possible for me to contemplate it at all without disintegrating into the formless abyss of Nietzsche's murdered God.

I have also been profoundly influenced by the work of the Belgian philosopher of sexual difference, Luce Irigaray, who argues that the Nietzschean death of God is an opportunity for women to birth God or the gods anew in our world. Irigaray's references to the divine are ambiguous and difficult to categorize, but from my own theological perspective she has helped me to see that our language about God needs to encompass fecundity, celebration and incarnation in a transformed and revitalized passion for the divine goodness of creation and the body. The Christian tradition, particularly Protestantism but also to a certain extent Catholicism, has developed an idea of a morally austere, distant and punitive God modelled on the image of the stern father figure of the patriarchal social order. Today, feminist theologians experiment with different ways of speaking about God – as mother, friend, creative spirit, nature, life and breath. Such forms of expression remind us that, even while respecting the unfathomable abyss of God, it is important to speak a language of faith that communicates joy, creativity, nurture and abundance, as well as unspeakable mystery. These different kinds of theological language are sometimes referred to as apophatic and cataphatic respectively. The cataphatic entails a profusion of imagery and language, which celebrates the all-encompassing presence of God in creation, while the apophatic recognizes the ultimate impossibility of speaking of God at all.

Because of my quest for a theological language that can express maternity as well as mystery, I refer to the Church in the feminine. Until the Second Vatican Council, Catholicism retained the earliest Christian understanding of the Church as a living and nurturing maternal body, symbolically associated with Eve as mother of the living, with Christ as eucharistic body, and with Mary as mother of Christ. I shall return to this theme later, but I have decided that, whatever the risks inherent in over-emphasizing the maternal dimension of the Church, I do not want to substitute 'it' for 'she' when referring to the most potent and widespread symbol of maternity in Western history.

I spent several years in an evangelical church when my children were young, and there I encountered a very different language of faith from that of the Catholic mystics. In that church, whatever the mystery of God, Jesus was apparently a vivid and undeniable presence. He told people things, held conversations, gave signs, answered prayers, and seemed to demand an absolute, unflinching and rather noisy loyalty in return. The problem was, I did not know him, or I did not know what people meant when they asked if I knew him. The more they offered to pray for me, the more perplexed I became. I doubt if any of them interpreted my conversion to Catholicism as an answer to prayer, but if I have in any sense discovered or begun to know Christ, it is through the sacramental and social vision of Catholicism.

The Catholic Church called to me and continues to attract me because she does not ask for simplistic language or unquestioning faith, although she can accommodate both. She offers what for me is a more credible Christ – a Christ who is intellectually satisfying and socially and materially nurturing. The Christ of the Catholic faith is sacramental mystery made intimate, tangible and earthy in bread and wine, in ritual and candlelight, in art and architecture, in politics and society, in a community of faith that encompasses all humankind in some form or another, and still sees God's grace in the natural world. Catholicism continues to offer that elusive glimpse of something understood, something expressed and communicated through the centuries by a certain language, a certain vision, a certain way of seeing the world.

This sense of recognition came to me when I was confined to hospital during my fourth pregnancy. A retired Presbyterian minister visited me and brought me books to read. They were all by Catholic authors, and they included Thomas Merton's *Seeds of Contemplation*. As I read, I began to realize that there were ways of speaking about Christ that were more compelling to me than the biblical literalisms of evangelical Christianity. Soon after my son was born, I went to see a priest and a year later I was received into the Catholic Church. That is the matrix in which this book was nurtured, and in which my own spiritual quest has developed.

'How can you write a book about Rome when you only spent ten days there?' somebody asked me. But the Rome in this book is as much a place of the imagination and the spirit as of the physical world. On my return to Bristol, I spent several months reading and researching about the city's art, architecture and history, and then went back for a few days to check up on certain details, so I hope that it is a travel guide of sorts. But unlike other travel guides that claim to offer an original view of a city, this rarely deviates from the beaten track of the tour guides. Instead, it seeks to bring an original vision to bear on the old, familiar places, so that perhaps by changing the way we look we also change what we see. I have chosen and arranged the material to form a theological narrative of Catholic history, so that I link places together not because of their physical proximity but because of their symbolic resonances.

I had a sense as I travelled about the city and read about it afterwards, that I was listening to voices that have shaped my thoughts over many years, and particularly during recent years of intense study. I wanted to acknowledge those voices and their influence on my ways of thinking and believing, so this is part personal reflection and part theological enquiry in conversation with other theologians and theorists. Readers familiar with the book based on my doctoral thesis, *God's Mother, Eve's Advocate*, will recognize common themes and resonances. However, this is not intended to be an academic treatise, and I use endnotes only to give references for quotations. It is primarily a discursive ramble along the highways and byways of Catholic history and culture, gathering together the fragments of the past and attempting to shape them into a pattern for the present and a vision for the future. It is an exploratory and tentative quest for meaning, and like every pilgrimage it is multilayered.

It is also a consciously gendered narrative, in so far as I decided not to occupy the place of the neutral, detached observer but to look for the story of woman encoded in the Catholic faith. I ask how a woman might learn to walk the Catholic way to God, without stumbling and perhaps dying along the way because of the load she must carry on her back. I am conscious of the many women who have set out along this path with such hope and inspiration, only to find themselves physically or metaphorically imprisoned by the men who have constructed barbed wire fences, funeral pyres, torture chambers and prison cells along the road to heaven. How can one be a Catholic and a feminist, a traditionalist and a postmodernist, a conservative and a radical, a believer and an agnostic, without tearing oneself apart in the process?

Or are these the wrong questions, questions that are already defined by and in captivity to a vision of being and becoming which is 'his' rather than 'hers', history rather than herstory? Must a woman make these violent and painful choices, and do they not always involve severing some part of ourselves that we cannot live without? Maybe there are hidden pathways and secret alleys that might allow us to link up the fragmented and incoherent dimensions of our modern world, and to weave together visions in which heaven and earth, God and the world, woman and man, nature and culture, can coexist without competition and violence, in relationships of mutual love and illumination.

With such possibilities in mind, Eve became my travelling companion, like the imaginary friends of early childhood. She is a wayward wanderer in the wilderness of history and culture, a once and future voice of wisdom and rebellion, of seduction and promise. Far more than her distant daughter and namesake, the Virgin Mary, the New Eve, it is the old Eve who symbolizes Everywoman's story in the Catholic Church.

Thus, playing truant from the Pontifical Conference, Eve and I went on a pilgrimage through Rome, and this is our story. I hope that others might find in it resonances of their own struggles and their own visions, wherever they belong in relation to this vast travelling roadshow called the Catholic Church that has trundled its way through the pages of history with such flamboyance, violence and beauty.

So come with me and taste and touch and see. Look at the shimmer of sunlight on an angel's wings, depicted in mosaic high above the altar of an ancient church. Close your eyes and breathe the incense-laden air with its waxy aura of a million candles flickering with the hopes and fears of all the generations of Christians. Reach out and let your hand linger on the well-worn foot of a beloved saint, as the Roman matrons crowd around you with their shopping bags, kissing and clucking and muttering and crossing themselves, praying for who knows what secret dream or frustrated desire burning within them? See the human form called forth from stone and wood and clay, evoking the divine among us. Let your mind unfurl and your body delight in this incarnate mystery, God with us, God of incense and candlelight, God of the vaulted dome and the musty sepulchre, God of the city streets and the laughing children, God of the mamas and the madonnas and the lithe young men who swagger around the Spanish Steps. God of the middle-aged woman who stands on the corner of the Via Appia, waiting for customers. God of the refugee mother and child who beg inside a church until the priest comes and chases them away. God of the butchery and murder of history, God of the corruption and decadence of Rome, God of the manger and God of the cross. Come with me. I cannot show you God, but I can show you the pointers, the arrows, the markers, and there, in between, in the silent gaps, maybe we will sense the absence that is not God, and maybe that absence is the closest that we can come to the presence of God.

Notes

1. See Victor Turner, *Dramas, Fields, and Metaphors: Symbolic Action in Human Society* (Ithaca, NY, and London: Cornell University Press, 1974).
2. Catherine of Siena, *The Dialogue*, trans. with introduction by Suzanne Noffke, O.P. (Mahwah NJ: Paulist Press, 1980), p. 364.
3. Thérèse of Lisieux, *The Autobiography of Saint Thérèse of Lisieux: The Story of a Soul*, trans. John Beevers (New York: Doubleday, 1989), p. 147.

Creation of Adam, Michelangelo, Sistine Chapel

In the Beginning:
The Sistine Chapel

Creativity, visions and symbols

In a mighty act of creation, God reaches down through the heavens, swirling high above our heads, summoning a world out of the darkness and the depths. We stand in shadows far below, shades of pink and brown and yellow, faces straining upwards, forbidden cameras flashing, a babel of languages despite the repeated requests for silence over the loudspeaker.

No reproduction can do justice to the ceiling of the Sistine Chapel, to that sense of being part of a huddle of earthed humanity dwarfed by the enormity of God's and the artist's creative power. Michelangelo's genius was described by one of his contemporaries, Giorgio Vasari, as 'divine rather than earthly'. The ceiling of the Sistine Chapel transforms the material elements of plaster and paint into a translucent membrane thinly stretched between time and eternity, heaven and earth. The artist not only represents the story of creation but recreates it in such a way that it becomes something continuous, forever happening above us and around us. The artist becomes the co-creator. The creature creates the Creator anew.

But Michelangelo's masterpiece is a reminder that even the greatest and most original artistic achievement is a product of its time and place, for he views the story of Genesis through a particular cultural lens that obscures many of its original features. By comparing what Genesis says with what Michelangelo sees, we begin to understand the ways in which texts come to be defined and distorted by their contexts. When we enter an era such as our own, when the old meanings have disintegrated and we stand in need of new spiritual visions and narratives, it is sometimes helpful to insert ourselves imaginatively into that gap between texts and their contexts. From such a position, shuttling between the text and its interpreters, we can begin to weave different themes into the human story by taking up the threads of the past and using them to create new possibilities and patterns.

To say this is not to suggest that there is an inspired vision that gives us access to some pure purpose of being, before and beyond the meanings within which history enfolds human existence. We cannot peel back the layers of language, culture and experience to find an original self or an original god outside the tangled stories we inhabit. We are no less culturally conditioned than Michelangelo and his contemporaries, but our questions and struggles arise out of a different context. For many women today, that context is one that has been implicitly or explicitly shaped by feminism, so that we find ourselves asking what it means to be a woman, and how our self-understanding is affected and even dominated by the expectations and norms of masculine cultural and religious values.

This means that we are living through a time of exploration, which can be frightening and disorientating as well as exciting and challenging. No longer able to see ourselves reflected in the mirrors of history, women today are searching for symbols that give more authentic expression to our experiences, hopes and fears. Ursula King describes this as 'showing one's face, seeing a vision and finding a voice of one's own to proclaim it'.[1]

We cannot escape this dilemma simply by inventing new symbols, for by their very nature symbols are signs pregnant with history and promise, and they acquire their potency by their capacity to act as prisms, revealing shared worlds of meaning. We do not make symbols entirely in our own image, for their symbolic potency also comes from their capacity to make us in their image. That is why both Eve and Mary retain their cultural power to shape images of women in Western society, long after the Catholic Church has lost her religious power. Recognizing the crisis this represents in terms of theological language and worship, Constance Fitzgerald refers to feminists being 'imprisoned in a night of broken symbols'.[2]

We have to learn to read our symbols differently, to break open their meanings so that they can reveal new worlds, and one way of doing this is by exploring their histories and questioning the ways they have been interpreted. This means neither denying the claims of the past as postmodernists would have us do, nor being bound by its conventions as traditionalists would have us be, but rather creatively appropriating it so that it becomes the servant rather than the master of the future.

This is a form of recollection that requires hope as well as memory, for we must envision what we seek to become, before we can interpret what we have been. In order to remember creatively, we must view the past with a sense of expectation and use it as a map for exploring the unknown land of the future. But like ancient cartographers, we must expect constantly to redraw the maps of the past, as we chart the contours of the future worlds we travel towards. These paradoxes are beautifully summed up in T. S. Eliot's poem, 'East Coker', which suggests that 'In order to possess what you do not possess, / You must go by the way of dispossession.'

As a woman who came to feminist consciousness relatively late in life, that sense of dispossession has become the gateway to a journey of discovery into a new way of being. Eliot describes the painful dying to an old self positioned and constrained by a passing world and the awakening to a life that asks 'who am I?' and recognizes that the question is infinitely richer than any possible response.

So my quest for a feminist future begins with that ancient myth of human sexual origins, the story of Genesis. As I set out on this journey towards the unknown, I position myself bodily and imaginatively in the creative space between men's fantasies and women's dreams, between the concrete visions that men have inscribed across the face of history in this most enduring and symbolic of Christian cities, and the barely articulated longings of women that have yet to be fulfilled and expressed in the achievements and monuments of culture. Like every pilgrimage, this is a journey that involves an inner struggle with myself, the world and God, but it is also a journey of hope. I hope that for myself and for those who travel with me it will be a pilgrimage that deepens rather than destroys faith. As a woman in search of her God, I am exhilarated and inspired, not defeated and dismayed, by the majesty, daring and beauty of what man has achieved in the search for his God, in this city where the human and the divine encounter one another in the myriad visions of the Christian faith.

Male and female they created them

There are two creation stories in the Book of Genesis. The earlier version in Genesis 1 describes the creation of the sexes as simultaneous: 'God created man in the image of himself, in the image of God he created him, male and female he created them' (Genesis 1:27). Although this does not suggest a sexual hierarchy in the order of creation, it already raises a question that has shaped Christian attitudes and institutional structures for two millennia. What does it mean to be human made in the image of God? Is the Genesis reference to God as 'he' simply a literary convention with no theological significance, or does it already imply some primacy to the male? In other words, is woman made in the image of God or is she, as Thomas Aquinas argued from Aristotle, a 'defective male' so that God is only imaged in the perfect human form – that of the man? Or, as some thinkers such as Augustine have argued, does the image of God refer not to the sexually differentiated body but to the rational mind, which is an attribute common to both sexes? Even so, Augustine could not quite bring himself to see both sexes as equally made in the image of God. Woman, he argued, could only image God in partnership with the man, whereas man could image God alone.

Yet when one returns to the original Hebrew of the Genesis story, this account of creation is richly suggestive and enigmatic, and its image of God is one that privileges neither sex. The word used for God in Genesis 1 is *Elohim*, a plural noun that can refer to different divinities. Elsewhere in the Old Testament, the same word describes the goddesses of the Canaanite religions. To translate Elohim in the singular masculine is to betray a cultural prejudice by which male characteristics are projected onto God, even when the scriptural text resists such unambiguous positioning. When women today protest against this bias towards masculinity, we are being more rather than less faithful to the integrity and promise of the biblical tradition. Women and men together are made in the image of God, who is obscurely worshipped in all the gods and goddesses of the world's ancient and modern religions, while never being reduced to or confined by these human projections.

But whatever the nuances of Genesis 1, it is hard to find a single work of art that depicts this account of creation. The Christian artistic imagination has been captured by the second account of creation in Genesis 2 in which God creates Eve from Adam's rib, and it is this that provides the inspiration for Michelangelo's art and for countless other paintings. Genesis 2 invites contemplation of two separate creative acts through which God brings the male and female human being into existence, and Michelangelo depicts these in two of the most famous images in the Sistine Chapel. Unwittingly perhaps, these paintings tell us much about Christian perceptions of sexual difference, which are still relevant today.

Christians from the time of St Paul have looked at the Genesis story through cultural lenses shaped by patriarchal and male-centred or androcentric perspectives, and these distort the picture. Male biblical interpreters have seen social and sexual hierarchies written into the order of creation, so that Eve's creation from Adam is taken as evidence that God willed woman to be subordinate to man. Thinkers such as Augustine and Aquinas argued that such hierarchies are part of the created order of the world, even although in heaven all human beings will be perfectly equal. This idea was part of the official teaching of the Catholic Church until the middle of the twentieth century, so that in the theology of marriage the wife was subordinate to the husband despite being his spiritual equal. In theory, there has been a significant shift in Catholic doctrine since the 1960s, with an increasing emphasis on the equality in difference of the sexes. Yet as long as women remain excluded from positions of influence and authority in the Church, it remains debatable whether this constitutes a genuine change of heart in the Catholic hierarchy.

The idea that Genesis 2 supports the concept of woman's subordination in the order of creation is hard to defend, and indeed one could argue that, on the contrary, the creature becomes ever more refined as the creation moves to its climax in Eve. If Adam is not subordinate to the earth from which he was made nor to the creatures made before him, there is no reason why Eve should be subordinate to the body from which she was made, nor to the human creature who was made before her. The text suggests not domination but delight and mutuality in Adam's welcome of Eve as 'bone from my bones, and flesh from my flesh!' (Genesis 2:23). The woman's domination by the man comes about as a consequence of the Fall, and it therefore reflects not the original order of creation, but the sinful disordering of relationships, which comes about as a result of human rebellion against God. God says to the woman after the Fall, 'Your yearning shall be for your husband, yet he will lord it over you' (Genesis 3:16).

In fact, the idea of women's subordination to men in the Christian community becomes a persistent theme only after the conversion of Rome in the fourth century. Christianity has never been free from patriarchal influences, with the Pauline epistles already showing signs of sexual inequality in the Early Church. But early Christianity attracted women because of its egalitarian message of salvation and its marital ethos, which demanded mutual fidelity and respect between husbands and wives. Among Christian writers of the first four centuries there is a recognition that redemption entails Eve's liberation from the curse of marital domination in Genesis, and virginity is presented as a redeemed way of life that frees women from the demands of marriage and domesticity. Feminist scholars such as Elisabeth Schüssler Fiorenza and Anne Jensen have demonstrated that women had considerable influence and authority in the Early Church, even if this never amounted to full equality with men.[3]

Gradually, however, the mind of the Church became moulded around the contours of a society governed and controlled by men of power, and women found themselves once again relegated to positions of subordination and silence in a community that had at first promised so much. When we look at Michelangelo's representation of the sexes, we see the ambiguity of Christian attitudes to women reflected in his work.

Gender, love and solitude

Michelangelo was a visionary, an innovative artist who ultimately came into conflict with the Church authorities. The continuing power of his art suggests something of the prophetic, in so far as it evokes the presence of the divine for generations far removed in time from his own. But Michelangelo's representation of creation and the fall is a work that conforms to and indeed perpetuates in new forms the sexual stereotypes of the Christian tradition. To stand beneath that masterpiece as a woman and ask 'Who am I? Who is God? What relationship does my image bear to the divine image?' is to be drawn into a world of tensions and contradictions. There is ambivalence and apprehension in the mind of the creator – the artist and the artist's God – about this creature called woman. Tenderness vies with trepidation, divine genius is girded about with masculine anxiety, and the result is a troubling comment on the Christian view of woman, in our own time no less than in Michelangelo's time. One senses this even before entering the doors of the Vatican, when despite the abundance of naked female bodies depicted within, women are stopped and asked to cover their shoulders. The men of the Church are more comfortable with the female body as an artistic fantasy in the mind of its male creator than with the disturbing immediacy of the flesh.

In the Sistine Chapel, Michelangelo's God is an old man with a beard. Noel O'Donoghue, in his book on prayer, *Heaven in Ordinarie*, writes that Michelangelo 'shows the making of Adam as an expression of the Divine power: there is no compassion in the face of the creator'.[4] For O'Donoghue, this is a misrepresentation of the compassion of the biblical God in the act of creation. God, like any true artist, 'brings his material compassionately to fuller being, compassionately, for his own heart and mind is involved in the process. And how patiently and pathetically all things wait for the transformations of the art that awakens them to form and beauty.'[5]

By one of those strange quirks we may or may not call coincidence (surely coincidence is only the event that I have chosen not to weave meaningfully into the pattern of my life?), the morning I read that particular chapter I received a postcard from a friend entitled *Creation of Adam*. It depicts God as a maternal figure, crouching over the young Adam and cradling his head between her hands. It is an image full of tenderness and compassion, which seems much closer to O'Donoghue's understanding of creation than Michelangelo's distant, patriarchal God.

The creation of Adam is a tantalizing image. Adam, vulnerable and yearning, but with the physical perfection of a Greek god, reaches out languorously towards the outstretched finger of God. It has been argued that Michelangelo's work reveals his homosexuality, and it is hard for the modern viewer not to see homoerotic desire in the longing of Adam for God. But the painting also communicates something of the primal vulnerability of the human alone in the world. The small space between God's hand and Adam's seems to represent the insatiable longing of the human condition, the sense of reaching out for a God whom one can never touch, because one can never quite reach far enough to bridge that gap and feel the source of life, hand to hand and skin on skin. From now on Adam is forever destined to pine for a God who will always be just beyond reach, but so close, a few millimetres away in all eternity. This is the fundamental loneliness of every human being who yearns for a God who beckons from just beyond the fearful horizon, which is the mark of our finitude, inscribed upon the imagination of the mortal human being separated from but capable of desiring the infinite.

In Hebrew, the word used for the first human is *ha'adam*, a generic word most accurately translated as 'groundling' or 'earthling'. Pope John Paul II, in a reflection on Genesis, interprets this as the existential loneliness of every person, male or female, which is ontologically prior to but chronologically simultaneous with the coming into being of sexual difference.[6] In other words, the two creation stories in Genesis can be read together as meaning that sexual difference is an original feature of our humanity, but each of us is also the original human, the *ha'adam*, so that our humanity is not entirely defined by our sexual identities even if it is never free of these.

From the time of Augustine, Western and Eastern Christianity have had different interpretations of the significance of sexual difference. In the Eastern Church, it is believed that there were two stages of creation – a spiritual stage, which constitutes the ultimate reality, and a second, material stage, which included the creation of the sexed human body. This material creation was prior to the Fall and was therefore also good, but it anticipated the Fall and the coming of death into the world, and so the body was provided with the means for procreation. But in Christ the human being escapes the cycle of birth and death, and sexual difference ceases to have any enduring significance.

With Augustine, however, Western theology began to follow a different trajectory. Augustine argued that there was only one creative act and that the sexed human body was part of this. Because the redemption of the world in Christ brings about a new and everlasting creation, this means that our sexuality has eternal significance even for the resurrected body. So although Augustine is often and perhaps justifiably reviled by feminists for some aspects of his theology, he can also be credited with introducing the idea that the female body has its own eternal value and meaning. According to this understanding, sexual difference is not an afterthought but is part of what it means to be human, in the beginning, and it signifies our essential relation-ality. Man and woman are made for each other, for mutual self-giving in love. But at the same time, the human condition is also marked by a primal sense of solitude, and *ha'adam*, the groundling alone and without a companion among the beasts of creation, symbolizes this solitude before God.

Such loneliness is not gendered. Being a woman does not make one less aware of the abyss that opens up, often in the darkest, quietest part of the night or when faced with suffering and death. There are times when we feel reduced to a condition of abandonment and loss, condemned among all the creatures of the universe to be capable of imagination, anticipation and the dread of not being. Writers like Jean Paul Sartre and Albert Camus identify this as the existential angst of the human condition. It is the claustrophobic bearing down of infinity upon the finite, the leering face of nothingness, which lurks unseen but not unfelt around the corner of every moment of life. Even so, is it possible that this loneliness is nevertheless experienced in a more potent way by men than by women? Do the relationships and emotional engagements that surround women's lives provide some lessening of that inner solitude, some protection against the terror of the void?

Images of God

Gender theorists tend to speak today of sexual difference in terms of masculine autonomy and independence, and feminine relationality and interdependence. Psychologists such as Carol Gilligan argue that our cultural conditioning instils in us different characteristics and ethical values according to our sex.[7] Women grow up believing that we have an ethical duty to put others before self, and we tend to see the preservation of relationships and care for those around us as more important than developing a sense of individual identity and ethical autonomy. Men, on the other hand, are conditioned to value independence and individualism. They are likely to put principles before relationships, individual rights and freedoms before emotional needs and vulnerabilities, and they tend to see dependence on others as a sign of weakness. Some psychologists such as Nancy Chodorow suggest that this difference between feminine relationality and masculine individualism arises out of the experiences of early infancy.[8] The solitude of the masculine subject is a consequence of the early imperative for the male child to distance himself from the mother and model himself upon a father who is often absent. He must form his masculine identity in opposition to the mother who cares for and nurtures him, by identifying with a father figure whom he associates with distance and inaccessibility. Does Michelangelo's painting suggest the pathos of the father–son relationship, in Adam's lonely yearning and God's self-distancing power? To what extent has this primal psychological affliction visited itself upon centuries of theology, so that the Christian subject has come to be understood as the solitary male individual struggling to model himself upon a distant and powerful father God?

But Michelangelo's depiction of Eve suggests a very different reality, a different way of coming into being in the world, which seems to affirm some of our modern insights about the psychology of sexual difference. God does not create Eve from the heavens, and she does not reach up to a transcendent and distant God as she emerges from the side of Adam. She discovers herself in a world where God stands face to face with her upon the earth. His hand does not point towards her in creative power, but seems to beckon to her to arise and meet his gaze. Here, we see something of the compassion that O'Donoghue says is lacking in the creation of Adam. In fact, in Michelangelo's story of creation, God seems to come closer and closer to identifying with the creation, so that it begins with the turbulent swirling of a mighty and remote God in the heavens, and culminates in God's earthly intimacy in the creation of Eve.

From the cults of the ancient goddesses to modern religious feminism, women's sense of the divine has focused more on immanence than transcendence, more on a God who is to be found in the matter and life of creation than in abstract theological concepts. Women's forms of religious expression tend to celebrate fecundity, birth and harvest rather than sacrifice, death and bloodshed. This is perhaps not surprising, given that it is the female body that gives birth, nurtures and bleeds according to the rhythms and cycles of the natural world. It is harder for women than for men to escape our physical affinity with nature, and perhaps this is why women find a bodily, vulnerable God more credible and loveable than an omnipotent, transcendent deity. I think this difference is manifest in Michelangelo's two images of creation. There is a world of theological difference between the creation of Adam and the creation of Eve in these images. If Michelangelo's Adam and Eve could speak of the God they encounter in their first moment of being, would they not use very different language and concepts? Only together might they begin to form some understanding of the totality of God's presence – a God who reaches out from heaven but also stands upon the earth, a God who can seem remote, transcendent and powerful, but a God who can also seem close, immanent and vulnerable. Eve has much to tell Adam about God, but Adam's sons have yet to listen. Women theologians are still often locked in battle with their male counterparts about whose version of God is the right one.

But already, in the beginning, Michelangelo's male God seems ambivalent about the woman whom he gazes at so lovingly. The expression on God's face is quizzical, suggesting apprehension as well as tenderness. Is this a God who is already identifying the woman with the destruction of his masterpiece? There is a suggestion of reluctance in Michelangelo's God, an uncertainty about the wisdom of creating this woman who stumbles from Adam's body and lurches imploringly towards him. Maybe Eve is already begging for mercy, already pleading with God not to blame her for what lies ahead.

This possibility is strengthened when we look at the face of the woman who is held under God's arm in the creation of Adam. There is some uncertainty about who this woman represents. It has been suggested that she could be Eve, already created in the mind of God when Adam is created, or she could be Wisdom, Sophia, who in the Book of Proverbs says of herself that 'Yahweh created me when his purpose first unfolded, before the oldest of his works' (Proverbs 8:22). Mary has traditionally been identified with Sophia, so that the woman could even be the anticipatory presence of the Mother of God in creation. But however we interpret this enigmatic figure, it is an image that suggests woman's primal intimacy with God, and she gazes out towards Adam from God's protective embrace more in trepidation than in desire. She looks startled, as if sensing that this moment will bring her suffering rather than joy, alienation from rather than closer union with God.

Sexuality and the Fall

Theologians have debated over whether or not there would have been sex in Eden if there had been no Fall. Augustine initially thought not, because until death came into the world there would have been no need for procreation. Eve, therefore, must have been created as a companion, not as a sexual partner, for Adam. Later in life, however, Augustine decided this could not be so, for if God had intended to create a companion for Adam, surely he would have created another man? Therefore, concluded Augustine, the woman was created for sex and motherhood in the beginning, but had the Fall not happened, sex would have been a rational, deliberate act. I have never quite worked out whether this controlled lovemaking would be the equivalent of, say, washing one's hands, or going for a long walk in the country with a beloved companion. Both are rational and controllable acts, but as metaphors for sex they suggest somewhat different attitudes and experiences.

For Augustine, the fact that sex is subject to passions and desires that overwhelm reason and, moreover, give certain parts of the body a life of their own beyond the control of the mind, confirm that our sexuality is intrinsically sinful because of the Fall. Augustine, who famously prayed 'Lord, make me pure and chaste, but not yet', had a particularly strong libido, which he indulged freely in his younger days. The fact that he interprets the uncontrollability of erections as evidence of the inherent sinfulness of sex suggests the extent to which male experience has shaped the Christian understanding of sin. Nevertheless, Augustine implanted the idea in the mind of the Western Church that sexual pleasure is tainted by original sin and can only be justified if it is for the purposes of procreation. Beyond all the rationalizations of the Church's present teaching on birth control, I suspect there lurks this ancient belief that if women allow themselves the pleasure of sex, they must also pay the price.

Perhaps reflecting the trend to speculate about sex in Eden, Michelangelo seems to suggest *coitus interruptus* – the sexual bliss of Paradise forever interrupted by the distracting presence of the serpent. There is a bold sexuality hinted at in the image of Eve's temptation. Adam stands over her as she reclines on the ground. She turns her head to take the fruit from the serpent, and yet were she to turn back towards Adam, she might take his penis in her mouth instead. There is a hint that sexual foreplay is frustrated and deferred by the Fall.

But Michelangelo's serpent is also female, and this is one reason why his depiction of the Fall is such a potent demonstration of Christian misogyny. Woman here becomes completely identified with sin, not just as the one who first yields to temptation but also as the tempter. And when we look at the faces of Adam and Eve after the expulsion, although both have aged, it is Eve's face that bears the terrible marks of sin – tormented and wizened, the wide-eyed young girl who gazed out from the protective embrace of God in the beginning has tumbled into the wilderness of her dereliction, estranged from God and blamed by the man whose creation she witnessed with such foreboding. Eve flees from Paradise with the words of the Church Fathers ribboning out ahead of her: 'You are the devil's gateway'; 'sin began from a woman'; 'depraved in the thoughts of her mind'; 'The foolish mother is the fountain of our miseries'; 'a nest and a cave for the accursed serpent'; 'an occasion of death to man'; 'perverted in mind'.

The New Eve

However, the patristic writers who described Eve in such derogatory terms were celebrating her redemption, not her condemnation. With the exception of Tertullian's description of Eve as 'the devil's gateway', each of the foregoing is balanced by a reference to Mary, the New Eve, in whom the old Eve is redeemed. There is a persistent message in patristic theology that, in the words of Augustine,

> [Christ] came then a man, to choose first the male sex; and being born of a woman, to console the female sex; as if speaking to them and saying: That you may know that no creature of God is bad, but that an evil pleasure perverts it, in the beginning when I made man, I made him male and female; I condemn not the creature which I made. See, I am born a man; see, I am born from a woman. It is not then the creature I made which I condemn, but the sins which I made not. Let

either sex see its own honor, and either confess its own iniquity, and either hope for salvation.[9]

This quotation suggests both the ambiguity and the promise of the Christian message for women. Augustine reflects the traditional belief that Christ was male because the man has primacy over the woman, but he also insists on the full and active participation of both sexes in redemption as well as in the Fall. Historically, however, the theological understanding of the relationship between Eve and Mary changed from one of complex and reconciling interdependency to one of irreconcilable opposition. In the Vatican II document on Mary and the Church, *Lumen Gentium*, the patristic saying, 'Death through Eve, life through Mary', is repeated, but now it stands unambiguously for Eve as a symbol of fallenness, and Mary as a symbol of redemption.[10] Gradually, Mary has been understood less and less as a woman in whom Eve and all women are redeemed, and more and more as a unique and privileged member of her sex. In the title of Marina Warner's book, Mary is 'alone of all her sex',[11] while all other women are identified with Eve – the fallen, depraved and sinful female flesh which must be controlled at all costs, for it represents a constant threat to men.

Augustine had to insist repeatedly that the female flesh was redeemed in the incarnation because the men of his time found it impossible to believe that women's bodies could be part of God's eternal plan. Although in principle this fundamental belief in the universality of salvation has endured, the female body occupies a space of exclusion in the Catholic Church, and today we rarely hear priests preaching as Augustine did on the goodness of the female flesh. While symbolically Mary represents woman created, redeemed and bodily assumed into heaven, this belief finds no expression in the liturgies and rituals of Catholic life. The female body has only negative significance. It defines what women cannot do – we cannot be ordained, we cannot preach at Mass, we cannot enter certain monasteries and other male sanctuaries. I think this is because the Catholic male mind is still not entirely convinced that our bodies are included in the story of salvation.

Today, a growing number of women are looking again at the figure of Eve, and we are beginning to rediscover her significance. Women scholars are gathering together the surviving fragments of women's writings on Eve through the centuries, and these offer a very different understanding from that found in men's texts. Hildegard of Bingen wrote in the twelfth century, 'When God created Adam, Adam experienced a sense of great love in the sleep that God instilled in him. And God gave a form to that love of the man, and so woman is the man's love.'[12] Christine of Pizan (1365–c.1430) strongly asserted Eve's equality in creation: 'There Adam slept, and God formed the body of woman from one of his ribs, signifying that she should stand at his side as a companion and never lie at his feet like a slave, and also that he should love her as his own flesh.... I don't know if you have already noted this: she was created in the image of God.'[13]

Later, women began to use the Genesis story in a highly polemical way to argue for women's rights. Jane Anger, a sixteenth-century English pamphleteer, argued: 'Then lacking a help for him, God, making woman of man's flesh that she might be purer than he, doth evidently show how far we women are more excellent than men. Our bodies are fruitful, whereby the world increaseth, and our care wonderful, by which man is preserved. From woman sprang man's salvation.'[14] Sojourner Truth, a nineteenth-century freed slave woman, preached:

> that little man in black there say
> a women can't have as much rights as a man
> 'cause Christ wasn't a woman.

Where did your Christ come from?
From God and a woman!
Man had nothing to do with Him.
If the first woman God ever made
was strong enough to turn the world
upside down, all alone
together women ought to be able to turn it
rightside up again.[15]

These extracts suggest what is at stake when women bring their insights and concerns to bear on the biblical texts, and they also reveal how diminished and one-sided the authoritative readings of Genesis are.

It is not necessary to see Mary and Eve in opposition, for they represent the promise and the reality of what it means to be a woman. Eve represents every woman who struggles to be 'mother of the living' in the wilderness of culture and history. She symbolizes the complexity and the vulnerability of our desire, the difficulties that women experience as wives and mothers, the hardships that women have suffered through sexual oppression, childbearing, poverty and alienation. Mary guarantees that God is with Eve in her suffering, and that her existence has meaning and purpose. The female body is graced with eternal beauty, hope and dignity, which neither man nor serpent can ever take from her, for it is held safe in the image and likeness of God. To quote Catherine of Siena again: 'You, eternal Trinity, are the craftsman: and I Your handiwork have come to know that you are in love with the beauty of what you have made, since you made of me a new creation in the blood of your Son.'[16]

In recent years a number of marginalized and oppressed groups have realized that the way to subvert the language of denigration is not to reject it, but to appropriate it. So 'black' used to be a term of racial abuse, but black people themselves have turned it into a symbol of pride and dignity. Homosexual people are increasingly using the word 'queer' as a way of affirming and celebrating their sexuality, thus divesting the word of its power to insult. In the same way, Christian women need to reclaim Eve and make her a symbol of women's courage, dignity and goodness in the eyes of God.

Eve and Mary together constitute the symbolic space of woman's existence in Christ and the Church, not as a choice between the whore and the virgin, but as a necessary duality which expresses history and eternity, time and transcendence. Mary, the New Eve, stands behind us in Paradise and before us in Heaven. Eve leaves the gates of Paradise to accompany us on our long journey through time, sharing our struggles, our hopes, our stories. She is the patron saint of women's histories, of the herstories that have yet to be told.

But for this other Eve to emerge as a subject of redemption rather than an object of scorn, we need to scrape away the male sexual anxieties that have accumulated around the Genesis myth over the centuries. Only then might we appreciate afresh its poetic subtlety and its potential as a constantly renewable resource of artistic and theological creativity.

Restoring the vision

In 1980 restoration work was begun on the frescoes in the Sistine Chapel. A work of art that had previously seemed shadowy and sombre was now revealed to be one of luminous colour and delicacy. The pollution of centuries had obscured the original masterpiece, and what art historians took as evidence of a darkening of Michelangelo's vision was shown instead to be the darkening effects of time. So with the Book of Genesis: its original subtlety has been overshadowed through the centuries by the accumulated mire of prejudice and misogyny. If the story of creation is to be rediscovered in its integrity, and if Eve in particular is to be appreciated as woman made in the image of God, then biblical interpreters need to undertake a slow and loving task of restoration, to clear away the accretions and ask anew what the text is saying to us.

Phyllis Trible, in her influential study of the Hebrew poetry of Genesis, describes it as a love story gone awry.[17] She reads it as a literary work of art, which evokes a created world in which there is joy and vulnerability, delight and frailty, a world suffused with eros. But with the Fall, eros is overwhelmed by death, and the original harmony of creation disintegrates into a world of oppositions, conflicts and oppressions. Life loses to Death.[18]

The Christian story tells us that in Christ, life has forever triumphed over death. But the story revealed in the Bible and in the person of Jesus is continued within the traditions and institutions of the Church and the world, like the performance of a great drama being played out upon the stage of history from the beginning to the end of time. As with any work of creative genius, this is a profound drama with complex and open-ended meanings. It invites many forms of interpretation and might even have many possible endings. Christians are called to hope, and this means believing that the story will end well. In the words of Julian of Norwich, 'All shall be well, and all shall be well, and all manner of thing shall be well.' But we also know that the story of the human in Christ and of Christ in the human is in many ways a tragedy, full of pathos and suffering as well as promise and hope. Christians have brought love and healing to many through the ages, but they have also brought violence, misery and oppression in the name of Christ.

The silencing and exclusion of women by the men of the Church is surely one of the great and ongoing scandals of a faith that in the beginning held out such hope of sexual and social equality. That is why I have chosen in this first chapter to focus on the story of creation and the significance of sexual difference. Irigaray argues that underlying all other forms of oppression and violence in our world lies the question of sexual difference.[19] We will never achieve peace on earth and peace with creation, she suggests, until we achieve peace between the sexes. This means confronting our failure to create a world in which women and men coexist in ways that are fully equal and truly different. Only when women as well as men reflect the image of God in every Church structure, institution, place of learning and sacrament, including the sacramental priesthood, will the Church be true to her vocation to proclaim the renewal of all creation in Christ and the restoration of the human creature to his and her place of original goodness in the image and likeness of God.

So let's wander out of the luminous shadows of the Sistine Chapel into the bright Roman sunshine, but let us take with us the image and memory of Eve as she first steps into the dawn of creation, face to face with God. Looking through her eyes, questioning and exploring with her, let us try to see the world anew, as if seeing it for the first time, by allowing the light and shadow of history and imagination to play across the face of this most ancient and modern of Christian cities, as Eve begins a pilgrimage in quest of herself. And maybe, as an ironic parting gesture to Michelangelo's female serpent, we can read Veronica Zundel's poem 'Deception', to entertain us as we go:

> In Eden's sun the woman basks,
> she works, plays, loves as each day asks
> and knows not she is God's mirror and sign;
> till, curving elegant his tail,
> the serpent (who is surely male)
> insinuates a lack of the divine.

'To be like God' – a worthy goal
for any self-improving soul,
an offer she, or man, can scarce disdain.
Poor Eve! Why won't she realize
right now she's able, strong and wise
with nothing but the choice of good to gain?

Yet still the priests perpetuate
the lie that led to Eden's gate
and raised the fiery sword our bliss to bar:
still women make the same mistake
and bow to some religious snake
who tells us we are not the gods we are.[20]

Notes

1. Ursula King, *Women and Spirituality* (Basingstoke: Macmillan, 1990), p. 2.
2. Constance Fitzgerald, OCD, 'Impasse and Dark Night', in Joann Wolski Conn (ed.), *Women's Spirituality: Resources for Christian Development* (Mahwah, NJ: Paulist Press, 1986): pp. 287–311, p. 304.
3. See Elisabeth Schüssler Fiorenza, *In Memory of Her: A Feminist Theological Reconstruction of Christian Origins*, 2nd edn (London: SCM Press, 1995); Anne Jensen, *God's Self-Confident Daughters: Early Christianity and the Liberation of Women*, trans. O. C. Dean Jr (Louisville, KY: Westminster John Knox Press, 1996).
4. Noel Dermot O'Donoghue, *Heaven in Ordinarie: Prayer as Transcendence* (Edinburgh: T. & T. Clark, 1996), p. 44.
5. Ibid., p. 45.
6. See John Paul II, *Original Unity of Man and Woman – Catechesis on the Book of Genesis* (Boston, MA: St Paul Books and Media, 1981).
7. See Carol Gilligan, *In a Different Voice: Psychological Theory and Women's Development* (Cambridge, MA, and London: Harvard University Press, 1993).
8. See Nancy Chodorow, *The Reproduction of Mothering: Psychoanalysis and the Sociology of Gender* (Berkeley, CA: University of California Press, 1978).
9. Augustine of Hippo, 'Sermon 190', quoted in Bertrand Buby, SM, *Mary of Galilee, Volume III, The Marian Heritage of the Early Church* (New York: Alba House, St Pauls, 1997), p. 190.
10. See *Dogmatic Constitution on the Church, Lumen Gentium*, in Austin Flannery, OP (ed.), *Vatican Collection: Vatican Council II, Volume 1, The Conciliar and Postconciliar Documents* (Dublin: Dominican Publications; New Town, NSW: E. J. Dwyer, 1992), pp. 350–426.
11. See Marina Warner, *Alone of All her Sex: The Myth and the Cult of the Virgin Mary* (London: Picador, 1990).
12. *Hildegard of Bingen: An Anthology*, ed. Fiona Bowie and Oliver Davies (London: SPCK, 1992), p. 108.
13. Christine de Pizan, *The Book of the City of Ladies*, trans. Earl Jeffrey Richards (New York: Persea Books, 1982), I.9.2; pp. 23–4, quoted in Gerda Lerner, *The Creation of Feminist Consciousness: From the Middle*

Ages to Eighteen-Seventy (Oxford and New York: Oxford University Press, 1993), p. 144.

14. Jane Anger, quoted in Lerner, ibid., p. 151.

15. Sojourner Truth, 'Ain't I a Woman?', in Julia Neuberger (ed.), *The Things that Matter: An Anthology of Women's Spiritual Poetry* (London: Kyle Cathie, 1992): pp. 18–19.

16. Catherine of Siena, *Dialogue*, p. 365.

17. Phyllis Trible, *God and the Rhetoric of Sexuality* (Philadelphia, OH: Fortress Press, 1978), p. 72.

18. Ibid., p. 74.

19. Cf. Luce Irigaray, *je, tu, nous: Toward a Culture of Difference*, trans. Alison Martin (New York and London: Routledge, 1993); *Thinking the Difference*, trans. Karen Montin (London: The Athlone Press, 1994).

20. Veronica Zundel, 'Deception', in Michele Guinness, *Tapestry of Voices: Meditations on Women's Lives* (London: Triangle, 1996): pp. 9–10.

The Colosseum

Fallen Empires, Holy Wars:
The Colosseum

The militant Church

A plain wooden cross stands on the spot of the emperor's podium in the Colosseum, former scene of some of the most violent spectacles laid on by the emperors for the people of ancient Rome. A guide explains to a group of American tourists that the cross symbolizes peace in a place associated with death and violence. It is a sign of Christian opposition to the death penalty and public execution, she says. Perhaps her comment is intentionally barbed. A man has just been executed in the United States, prompting international outrage and a protest from Pope John Paul II.

In the Catholic Church there is growing opposition to the death penalty, and under the papacy of John Paul II there has also been a dramatic shift to a more pacifist church. But the historical association between Christianity and violence is deeply rooted, and it will take more than one peace-loving pope to bring about a change in Christian consciousness. While in every age there have been pacifist Christians and movements such as the Quakers that have refused to countenance violence, there has also been a militaristic streak running through the Christian religion, which has made it a powerful ally of empires and repressive regimes. America is the largest military power in the world and the only Western nation that still regularly kills its own citizens in the name of law and order, but it is also a society in which professing Christians exert a significant influence across a range of political issues. The fact that these often include support for the death penalty and nuclear weapons, indicates the extent to which Christianity remains deeply implicated in the politics of militarism and oppression.

So after two millennia of Christian history, that cross in the Colosseum is an enigmatic and perplexing symbol which can be interpreted in several ways. For some it might represent the victory of the Church of Christ over imperial Rome, but for others it might represent an imperial Church that has perpetuated the ambitions and methods of Rome in conquering the world for Christ. In the words of John Ferguson: 'The historic association of the Christian faith with nations of commercial enterprise, imperialistic expansion and technological advancement has meant that Christian peoples, although their faith is one of the most pacifistic in its origins, have a record of military activity second to none.'[1]

How can we explain these contradictions and paradoxes? How did a peace-loving and persecuted minority scattered about the fringes of the Roman empire grow into a movement so powerful that it has killed countless thousands in the name of its crucified Christ?

Violence and the social order

The grandeur and social cohesion of ancient Rome was founded upon violence – not only the violence of military conquest, but also the violence of the games where beasts and humans alike were tortured and killed for the entertainment of the crowds. Thomas Weidemann argues that the Roman arena was a space that marked the boundary between culture and nature, life and death, human and non-human.[2] In this place, Rome declared its power over the natural world by making wild beasts fight to the death, creating an industry in which hundreds of thousands of animals were captured and transported to arenas all over the empire. Human beings who were already socially dead because they had put themselves outside the ordered ranks of Roman society – criminals, rebellious slaves, prisoners of war and Christians – were physically put to death, ensuring the cohesion of the social order through the elimination of outsiders. Often this involved lurid spectacles of torture and sexual abuse. Ultimately, the fate of the hapless victim might be decided by the crowd. In the gladiatorial fights, it was for the people to decide whether the gladiator should live or die. Thumbs up and he (or even occasionally she) survived; thumbs down meant death. But as the recent film *Gladiator* suggests, the gladiators were often regarded as romantic heroes, the distant precursors perhaps of the modern Hollywood star, whose image is invested with the glamour of violence and death.

The democratic involvement of the people was central to the social function of the games. They were displays of imperial munificence, when the emperor and rich citizens funded lavish spectacles for the entertainment of the masses. The Colosseum, originally known as the Flavian Amphitheatre, was built by the emperor Vespasian on the site of an ornamental lake in the former palace of the hated emperor Nero. Thus it was strategically positioned to win the favour of the people. When it was inaugurated in the year AD 80 by the emperor Titus, the celebration lasted one hundred days and involved the killing of 50,000 beasts and hundreds of gladiators. In addition to the extravagant violence of its spectacles, the building was an architectural achievement that has had a formative influence on Western architecture, and it has arguably never been rivalled in its perfect integration of form and function. Its massive scale signified the grandeur and apparent indestructibility of the

Roman empire and its emperors. Its arched entrances and tiered rows of seating made it capable of accommodating up to 50,000 spectators, in ranks reflecting the social hierarchy. Its arena could be flooded for the staging of mock sea battles. Under the arena, its corridors, cells and cages were designed to deal efficiently with the living and dead bodies of the people and animals who were used in the games.

The Colosseum seems to symbolize René Girard's theory that the primal bonds of the social order are created through the unifying power of violence and sacrificial bloodshed.[3] In a reinterpretation of Freud's theory of the Oedipus complex, Girard argues that our primary relationships are formed through the desire to model ourselves on others, whose disciples we become. However, our desire to be like them gradually gives rise to envy and aggression, so that the model becomes a rival to be eliminated. Intricately spread through all the complex networks of human relationships, these forces of desire and envy build up collectively until they reach an explosive level, and if they do not find controlled release, they have the power to unleash social disintegration and anarchy. Socially sanctioned violence such as religious sacrifice, war or blood sport, has a cathartic effect, allowing us to give vent to these forces of aggression and creating a sense of peace and well-being. Thus social bonds are temporarily restored, until the build-up of violence requires another sacrifice. The victim of such violence is usually a randomly chosen scapegoat – a group, an individual or an animal – onto whom the crowd projects its hostility, in such a way that the mob hides from itself the true nature of the violent act. Thus the scapegoat will be seen as guilty of some offence against society, the gods or fate, which justifies the violence and gives the perpetrators a sense of moral righteousness.

For a recent example, one might consider how suspected paedophiles became victims of mob violence in several British cities. The paedophile is a scapegoat onto whom society projects many of its darkest and most unacknowledged fears, but we conceal our violence even from ourselves by lending a sense of moral outrage to our actions, and attributing evil to the victim. One could also think of the latent aggression towards the growing number of asylum-seekers who flee from intolerable situations of persecution and poverty, only to find themselves subject to the more subtle torments of institutionalized racism and xenophobia in the Western democracies. In modern society no less than in ancient Rome, the moral order is founded upon violence and is sustained through the cultural if not the physical elimination of those who are deemed others and outsiders.

The popularity of the Roman games gradually dwindled during the fourth century, so that by the beginning of the fifth century they had virtually ceased. However, this was more to do with the declining fortunes of the empire than with the impact of Christianity.[4] Although early Christians had expressed concern about the games, their primary objection was not to do with the fate of the victims, but with the psychological damage to the spectators. Augustine set in motion a process that would influence Christian practice for two thousand years: there was no similarity between the secular city and the city of God. The Church's task was not to transform secular politics, but to transcend them. Thus Christians sought to protect themselves from contamination by the violence of the games, but they did not seek to eliminate the games even after the conversion of Rome.

Christians were martyred in the Roman arena and circus, but there is no evidence of any Christian deaths in the Colosseum itself. However, later accounts, embellished by Christian hagiographers, identify the Colosseum with the martyrdom of many Christian saints such as St Ignatius and St Sebastian, and the building has always occupied an ambiguous position in Christian culture. For many centuries it was allowed to fall into neglect and was plundered to provide building materials for Roman churches. During the Counter-Reformation, when the face of Rome was transformed by the triumphant reassertion of papal power and patronage, Bernini drew up plans to convert it into a massive church, but there were insufficient funds to implement his design.

In the eighteenth century the Colosseum became a motif for Romantic poetry and art. Christianity was no longer the central focus of European culture. Rome and Greece had come to symbolize a classical golden age, which had been brutally destroyed by Christianity. Lord Byron's poem 'Rome', carved into the plinth of his statue in the gardens of the Villa Borghese, suggests the nostalgia of the era, when Rome was invested with all the masculine fantasies and dreams of its heroic past:

> O Rome! my country! city of the soul!
>   The orphans of the heart must turn to thee,
> Lone mother of dead empires! and control
>   In their shut breasts their petty misery.
> What are our woes and sufferance? Come and see
>   The cypress, hear the owl, and plod your way
> O'er steps of broken thrones and temples, Ye!
>   Whose agonies are evils of a day –
>   A world is at our feet as fragile as our clay.
>
> Alas! the lofty city! and alas!
>   The trebly hundred triumphs! and the day
> When Brutus made the dagger's edge surpass
>   The conqueror's sword in bearing fame away!
> Alas for Tully's voice, and Vergil's lay,
>   And Livy's pictured page! – but these shall be
> Her resurrection; all beside – decay.
>   Alas, for Earth, for never shall we see,
> That brightness in her eye she bore when Rome
>   Was free!

Today, the dramatic impact of the Colosseum is diminished by the wide and crowded streets surrounding it – a legacy of yet another powerful dictator: Mussolini. Tourists throng around it, and hopeful young men dressed as gladiators shout angry warnings to those who take their photographs without paying. Stalls are veiled in gauzy scarves fluttering in the breeze, and street vendors offer wind-up toys, which crawl and squeak around the tourists' feet. The building broods solemnly around the noise and clutter, its derelict majesty attesting to the grandeur and frailty of human power, the glory and barbarity of human achievement.

I stand in its shadowy vaults, straining to hear some distant echo of the cries that surely must have seeped into the ancient stones, some whisper of the suffering inscribed in the building's past. But there is only the bright chirrup of the tour guides and the fretful grumble of tourists with blistered feet and heavy camera bags.

The building is so vast that one can always find a quiet niche away from the crowds, so I retreat to a refuge and try to look at the history and meaning of the place through a woman's eyes. Where does Eve belong in this human story dominated by male power, aggression and violence?

Genesis, sex and violence

If we are to retell the story of human origins and history, we need to consider the ways in which violence has been understood in relation to creation and the Fall. Is it possible to discover different readings that might transform our understanding of Genesis, so that violence rather than sex becomes the focal point of original sin and the fundamental predicament of the human condition? Such a vision would shift the locus of sin from the female flesh to the bloody wars and assaults of fallen masculinity.

The third and fourth chapters of Genesis describe two originating human acts that incurred God's wrath and condemned
humankind to suffering and exile. The first act is disobedience,
and the second is fratricide. Despite the fact that Christians have
always interpreted the Fall in sexual metaphors, there is no
suggestion in Genesis that the sexual relationship between Adam
and Eve is directly implicated in either the causes or the
consequences of sin. Indeed, contrary to the overwhelming weight
of the Christian tradition, the first direct biblical reference to sex
is a passing aside, which does not invest the sex act with any
particular moral or spiritual significance: 'The man had intercourse with his wife Eve, and she conceived and gave birth to
Cain' (Genesis 4:1).

It is through conception and motherhood, not through sexual
intercourse, that Eve finds herself entangled in the suffering and
loss that are the consequences of sin, for Eve's two sons were
humanity's first murderer and first murdered. Such a double loss
lays bare the anguish of Eve's exile from Paradise, the real
meaning of the words, 'you shall give birth to your children in
pain' (Genesis 3:16). It is the maternal truth behind Julia Kristeva's
lament:

> One does not give birth in pain, one gives birth to pain: the
> child represents it and henceforth it settles in, it is continuous.
> Obviously you may close your eyes, cover up your ears, teach
> courses, run errands, tidy up the house, think about objects,
> subjects. But a mother is always branded by pain, she yields to
> it. 'And a sword will pierce your own soul too...'[5]

When Eve gave birth to Cain and Abel, she gave birth to the
world's sorrow as well as to her own.

Genesis 4 tells the story of Cain and Abel and the murder of
Abel by Cain: 'Yahweh asked Cain, "Where is your brother

Abel?" "I do not know" he replied. "Am I my brother's guardian?" "What have you done?" Yahweh replied. "Listen to the sound of your brother's blood, crying out to me from the ground"' (Genesis 4:10).

There follows a process of curse and punishment, which mirrors many of the features of the earlier account of Adam's punishment. This raises the question as to what, in biblical mythology, constitutes the first act of human sinfulness? The Christian tradition has traced the fall back to the eating of the forbidden fruit, with the onus of responsibility falling primarily on Eve. But some Jewish exegetes offer a different interpretation of Genesis 3. Rabbi Jonathan Magonet writes:

> It is as if God, like an overprotective father, had accidentally achieved the very thing He wanted to avoid. By trying to keep the children from the pain of knowledge, God led them to seek it; in trying to keep them in the Garden of Eden, in the paradise of childhood, God had given them the impetus to step outside – and once outside, there was no way back.[6]

Magonet goes on to interpret the expulsion as a moment of liberation, when 'God cut the strings of the puppets and let them walk erect upon the earth.'[7]

Another Jewish scholar, Tikva Frymer-Kensky, offers a similar interpretation. She sees the eating of the fruit of the tree of knowledge as symbolizing the moment when humankind broke free of the tyranny of the pagan gods and accepted moral responsibility for a world in which we must live without recourse to divine intervention. Thus, in Frymer-Kensky's reading, Eve is a Promethean figure who 'wrests knowledge from the realm of the divine, takes the first step towards culture, and transforms human existence.'[8]

Honnor Morton, a nineteenth-century English nurse, also sees

Eve as a misunderstood figure who brings freedom and maturity to the human race. She writes:

> Hearken, O Eve, Mother of us all, greatest and grandest of women: you who have been maligned all down the ages, know at least that one of your daughters blesses you, and proclaims your choice good. To you, oh Eve, we owe it that we are as gods, and not as children playing in the garden – that we know the good and evil and are not left in ignorance and lust. Man had stayed ever in uninquiring peace, but to you was given strength to grasp the apple, to proclaim that woman at least prefers wisdom and the wilderness to idle lasciviousness in Eden.[9]

Such readings invite us to think differently about the nature and origins of sin. If the story of Adam and Eve in the garden represents the acquisition of moral knowledge and thus the maturing of humankind, then the first immoral act is not the eating of the fruit (one cannot be immoral before knowing good and evil), but the murder of Abel. This signifies the moral failure of humankind and the descent into violence and death.

The men of the Church have through the ages developed a theological culture of sin, temptation and death around the figure of Eve and her association with female sexuality, while neglecting Cain's violence and its association with male aggression and competitiveness. 'Yahweh looked with favour on Abel and his offering. But he did not look with favour on Cain and his offering, and Cain was very angry and downcast' (Genesis 4:5). Cain's primal resentment against his brother has haunted history, and perhaps beyond all men's wars about territory and ideology lurks this ancient sense of rejection. Yahweh, the patriarchal God, becomes a figure whose sons must vie for his attention and affection. But God not only curses Cain for killing Abel. God also puts a mark on Cain to protect him, saying that 'if anyone kills Cain, sevenfold vengeance shall be taken for him' (Genesis 4:15). When we repay violence with violence, we always bring sevenfold vengeance upon ourselves, our loved ones and our nations for generations to come.

Girard points out that Cain, the Bible's first murderer, also builds the first city.[10] Thus the biblical myth seems to share the insight that there is a close association between the formation of the social bonds of culture and the primal expression of murderous rivalry between human beings. But Girard also argues that Christ breaks this spiral of destructive desire and vengeance, by offering humankind a new model for discipleship. Christ is, he suggests, the ultimate scapegoat, and the gospels reveal for the first time the scapegoating mechanism, with their insistence that the victim is innocent and the crowd is guilty. Christ on the cross exposes sacrifice as a collective human act of violence against the love of God, and in the revealing power of his death he invites us to form new communities based not on aggression and violence but on forgiveness and love. Through his death, he offers humankind a chance to begin again by following a different way of relating and forming communities. But, argues Girard, because society remains trapped in the mechanisms of violence, those who follow Christ's peaceful example must themselves expect to become the scapegoats and victims of the social order. Society will not tolerate in its midst the one who threatens to expose its violent origins by refusing its rules of engagement.[11]

The scapegoat mechanism is a subtle and pervasive social force, and it is perhaps inevitable that Christianity has recognized this dimension of the crucifixion only in fleeting and often intangible ways. Christian theologies of the atonement – the forgiving and reconciling power of the crucifixion – have perpetuated images of an angry and vengeful God who demands and even takes pleasure in the suffering of his Son. God has been used to mask rather than to expose the violent origins of religious sacrifice in Christianity as in any other religion. Thus the idea of a wrathful and punitive God who must be placated by constant sacrifice has insinuated its way into Christian consciousness over the centuries, giving rise to a multitude of terrors and tyrannies that have fermented in the shadow of this absolute and ruthless deity. Gerard Hughes, in his popular book *God of Surprises*, describes a caricature of God as a monstrous tyrant called 'Good Old Uncle George' who lives in a basement and terrifies the children who come to visit him, to illustrate the truth that 'we can construct a God who is an image of our tyrannical selves.'[12]

Thérèse of Lisieux seems to have internalized an ethos of suffering we might well associate with the idea of a God who delights in pain, but she also recognized the need for a new vision and language of God, which would make love rather than justice the central theme of the incarnation. Thérèse writes, 'From the depths of my heart, I cried: "O my divine Master, must it be only Your justice which has its victims? Hasn't Your merciful love need of them too? It is everywhere rejected and ignored."'[13] This emphasis on merciful love rather than justice might move us in the direction of a Girardian theology of atonement, but it might also help us to listen anew to the message of the Early Church. If we have forgotten the social dimension of the revealing and reconciling love of the cross, it seems that the Early Church did recognize its significance and its challenge. One of the earliest descriptions of Christian life, the second-century 'Epistle to Diognetus', suggests a beatitudinal ethos in which the mimesis of Christ's non-violent love led to Christians becoming the scapegoats of a society founded upon and held together by violence:

> They love all men, and are persecuted by all. They are unknown, and they are condemned; they are put to death, and they gain new life.... They are dishonoured, and their dis-

honour becomes their glory; they are reviled, and are justified. They are abused, and they bless; they are insulted, and repay insult with honour. They do good, and are punished as evil-doers; and in their punishment they rejoice as gaining new life therein. The Jews war against them as aliens, and the Greeks persecute them; and they that hate them can state no ground for their enmity.[14]

This might be a rather idealized account, and one need only read Paul's second letter to the Corinthians to realize that the Early Church suffered many of the same tensions and problems as every other human community. But perhaps in this instance the image and the ideal spoke more powerfully than the reality of Christian life. If many Christians were apostasizing and partici-pating in all the hedonistic delights of Roman life, they were not the ones who were seen as the defining norm. It was the refusal of the few that defined the Church in the eyes of its enemies, and that created a culture of persecution and martyrdom.

How did this peaceful ethos relate to early readings of Genesis? If there is, as I have suggested, an intricate relationship between texts and their contexts, how did the context of the Early Church shape the understanding of scripture?

Genesis in the Early Church

Although the figures of Adam and Eve have been central to the Christian story from the first century, only gradually did Eve become invested with the sexual significance that she has today. The first Christians saw death rather than sex as the focal point of sin and vulnerability. Sex was implicated because it seemed to be inextricably bound up with the cycle of procreation and death. In societies where women die in childbirth, infant mortality is high, and life is often brief and painful, such ideas are hardly a sign of sexual repression. They are honest observations about the way things are.

In the Early Church, the virginal woman or man was a potent symbol of Christ's triumph over death, for in a world in which death has been overcome, procreation and the suffering associated with it are no longer necessary. In the order of redemption, virginity originally symbolized not sexual abstention but the defeat of death and the redemption of the body. In other words, the purpose of avoiding sex was to avoid perpetuating death through procreation – it was not to avoid the pleasures of the sex act itself.

The revolutionary attitude to death in the Early Church had two social consequences which caused considerable unease in the Roman empire. First, it meant that many Christians were unafraid of death and martyrdom and indeed welcomed the martyr's death with a zeal that some early Christian writers found distasteful. Thus the worst that Roman society could threaten – a hideous death in the arena – became for some Christians a form of suffering identified with the cross of Christ and therefore a glorious way to die. There was perhaps no more effective way to subvert a regime that retained control over its people by the threat of violence.

Second, believing as they did that the New Testament and the example of Christ required them to reject violence, the first Christians resolutely refused to participate in the militarism of the Roman empire. In an empire in which political and social bonds were sustained by violence, this relatively small group of pacifists posed a problem out of all proportion to its size. Ferguson writes that

> for something like a century and a half after the ministry of Jesus, Christians would not touch military service, and for more than another century the predominant sense continued

that Christianity and war were incompatible. Christians were charged with undermining the Roman Empire by refusing military service and public office; they answered that human life was sacred to them, and they were the race given over to peace, that God prohibits killing even in a just cause, without exception, that the weapons of the Christians were prayer, justice and suffering.[15]

In addition, Christians refused to bow down before the gods of the Roman empire. Rome was tolerant of religious diversity – in this it was perhaps not unlike our modern pluralist societies – but the Roman gods were political as well as religious figures, with the emperor himself being regarded as divine. To refuse to worship the gods was to militate against the prosperity and well-being of the empire, and this led to successive waves of persecution and martyrdom in the second and third centuries.

But the first Christians were appalled by the degradation and humiliation of the imperial cults, and their understanding of idolatry was closely associated with an affirmation of the dignity and freedom of the human being made in the image of God and redeemed in Christ. Thus the rejection of idolatry was in itself a rejection of religious violence and abuse.

Elaine Pagels, in her book *Adam, Eve and the Serpent*, explores the ways in which this early Christian culture of non-violence and religious resistance was related to interpretations of Genesis. She writes, 'for nearly the first four hundred years of our era, Christians regarded freedom as the primary message of Genesis 1–3 – freedom in its many forms, including free will, freedom from demonic powers, freedom from social and sexual obligations, freedom from tyrannical government and from fate; and self-mastery as the source of such freedom.'[16]

This has some resonances with Frymer-Kensky's understanding of Eve as the one who liberated humankind from the caprice and tyranny of the pagan gods. However, Pagels goes on to note that this interpretation changed with Augustine and the conversion of Rome:

> In a world in which Christians not only were free to follow their faith but were officially encouraged to do so, Augustine came to read the story of Adam and Eve very differently than had the majority of his Jewish and Christian predecessors. What they had read for centuries as a story of human freedom became, in his hands, a story of human bondage.... Adam's sin not only caused our mortality but cost us our moral freedom, irreversibly corrupted our experience of sexuality (which Augustine tended to identify with original sin), and made us incapable of genuine political freedom.[17]

It is perhaps not entirely coincidental that this great master of Christian theology, who linked sex and sin so inextricably together in the Christian imagination, was also the first to develop a Christian theory of the just war. Augustine made it possible for the first time for Christians to lend intellectual and moral justification to violence.

From pacifism to holy war

The Early Church used the rhetoric of warfare – even the word 'sacrament' derives from the Latin *sacramentum*, which is the military oath of allegiance sworn by Roman soldiers to the emperor – but this referred to the spiritual battle against evil. Christ had, in the words of Clement of Alexandria, summoned together 'his own soldiers of peace' to 'an army that sheds no blood'.[18] It is one of the more tragic twists of history that, after the conversion of Rome in the fourth century, such language increasingly became literal rather than figurative, making Christianity one of the most bellicose religions in world history.

But although Augustine was the first to offer a reasoned defence of Christian participation in war, it would be wrong to see him as the founding father of Christian militarism. His writing on war is an anguished attempt to think through what could at best be only a necessary evil, at a time when the structures of the empire were disintegrating around him. Justice was, according to Augustine, a more absolute value than peace, given that there could be peace without justice as in the case of the Pax Romana. War could be undertaken as an act of neighbourly love in defence of a third party but never in self-defence, since the Christian had nothing to fear from death. Moreover, in Augustine's bleak view of fallen human nature, war was an occasion of sin for all parties involved, and there could not be a glorious war or an untarnished hero. All alike stood under the judgement of God and were bound by the obligation of neighbourly love, and it was these two factors that informed his thinking on war. War was a sordid business and evidence of the sinful human predicament, but if the alternative was to turn aside from injustice against one's neighbour, then it was the lesser of two evils.

Far from advocating the idea of a holy war, Augustine desacralized war,[19] robbing it of its religious pretensions and its associations with divinity. In Girardian terms, this is a necessary stripping away of the guise of honour and divine sanction by which society has always sought to glorify violence. (One need only think of Margaret Thatcher's fury when the Archbishop of Canterbury refused to ring the church bells to celebrate Britain's victory in the Falklands War.) If the churches in Western society withdrew all their justification and prayer from the business of war, it is unlikely that they would continue to enjoy the much-vaunted tolerance of modern liberalism. As in Rome, Christian collusion in violence is the precondition for Christianity's acceptance by the state.

Until the Middle Ages Christians remained ambivalent about war, mindful of the fact that it did not conform to the teachings of Christ. The spilling of human blood was never really justified, and even as feudal war lords rode into battle, they had priests at home saying Masses for their souls and undertook elaborate penances on their return. It was with the crusades and the increasing violence of campaigns against those deemed enemies of the Church that war and bloodshed became marks of glory rather than shame on the Christian conscience. By the time that Thomas Aquinas was writing in the thirteenth century, war was an accepted part of Christian culture. Timothy George points out that Aquinas's *Summa* discusses war in one short chapter while devoting 24 long chapters to angels.[20] Aquinas also added the justification of self-defence to Augustine's theory, and today this remains one of the few acceptable reasons for going to war in the teachings of the Catholic Church.

Modernity and war

Despite its earliest convictions, Christianity has in practice achieved very little in terms of banishing war and violence from human relations. One could argue that the greatest moves towards non-violence have emerged in the post-Christian era of liberal democracy and human rights, but this in itself invites deeper reflection. If these political ideals have inspired people of all religions and cultures around the world, they have their origins in Judaeo-Christian beliefs about human equality, dignity and freedom. The modern secular democracies are rooted in the values of the Christian tradition, even if they have discarded the religious beliefs and practices that give coherence and substance to these values. Girard argues that resistance to violence in the Western democracies and the quest for non-violent forms of conflict resolution and law enforcement are in themselves the consequence of two thousand years of Christian influence. The post-Christian world, claims Girard, cannot escape the legacy of Christianity's rejection of the sacrificial shedding of blood. But in the aftermath of the Christian tradition, and with the absence of any ritualistic provision for sanctioned bloodletting (for example, through religious sacrifice), Western societies risk a descent into anarchy because of the unleashing of the powers of violence without any controlling mechanism.[21]

Those who claim that religion causes war would do well to look more closely at the legacy of the last hundred years. This was a century when the societies that fought the most terrible wars and unleashed the most appalling suffering were post-Christian societies, which had turned their backs on their Christian heritage in order to conform to new political and social ideologies. Stalinist Russia was an atheist communist state when it put to death some twenty million of its people. Nazism took root in a society that represented the apotheosis of Enlightenment ideals of culture, learning and tolerance – a society in which Jews had been assimilated after centuries of Christian persecution and marginal-ization. When America dropped atomic bombs on Hiroshima and Nagasaki, it did so for political and possibly scientific reasons in order to test its new weapons, not for religious reasons. In other words if religion causes war, why has the end of religion not meant the end of war in Western society?

Warfare has become progressively more barbaric and indiscri-minating, even as it has become more technologically efficient. In 1992 UNICEF's *State of the World's Children* report referred to the millions of children killed, disabled or rendered homeless because of war. It went on to say that

This 'war on children' is a 20th-century invention. Only 5% of the casualties in the First World War were civilians. By the Second World War the proportion had risen to 50%. And, as the century ends, the civilian share is normally about 80% – most of them women and children ... The time has now come for a worldwide public to cry out against this war on children – against those who use the weapons and those who supply them ... and insist that this appalling stain on the 20th century should not be allowed to seep over into the 21st.[22]

In this era of suffering children, perhaps the most bitter irony is that the world's five major arms producers are also the five permanent members of the United Nations Security Council. In recent years Britain and America – the world's two largest arms manufacturers – have become the self-appointed guardians of the new world order, with a series of bloody interventions in regions such as Iraq and the former Yugoslavia. Shares in the arms manufacturing industries soared during these conflicts, so that whatever these countries spend on their military escapades, they are likely to recoup through the arms trade. We do not create peace by profiteering from war, and history will surely judge these contradictions as one of the more extreme forms of global madness at the beginning of the third millennium.

Perhaps one of the darker legacies of 30 years of feminism is that women now regard it as their 'right' to fight in the front line alongside men. The presence of growing numbers of women in the military has exposed some of the deep cultural prejudices and stereotypes that surround war. The female body, associated with nurture and new life, chattel to be defended and protected from the enemy, wants to get up and go to war along with her men. Not only that, but violence and sexual aggression are often the hallmarks of so-called 'girl-power' in the media, so that sometimes the most conspicuous achievement of feminism seems to be the tendency of a growing number of young women to mimic masculine models of violent self-assertion. In cultures sustained and founded upon violence and the threat of violence, equality can perhaps only ever mean freedom to participate in that violence. If feminism is to achieve its goals, it is not enough to struggle for women's equality, we also need to struggle towards a culture of peace.

But the increasing problem of violence among women should not be allowed to obscure the fact that war and violence are overwhelmingly associated with male behaviour through the ages. Still today women are statistically many times more likely to suffer and die at the hands of men, whether directly through domestic abuse and sexual violence, or indirectly through war and political violence, than vice versa. By the same measure, men are victims as well as perpetrators of violence, but they are rarely victims of lethal violence by women. A recent British survey suggests that, although men and women both experience domestic violence, women's attacks on men seldom result in serious injury. By contrast, women and children are more likely to die at the hands of men in their own families than at the hands of strangers. Globally, nationally and domestically, the problem of violence is a male problem, however much it might involve the tacit collusion or co-operation of mothers, wives, sisters and daughters.

Envisioning peace

Resistance to violence can only be effective through an holistic vision of an alternative way of living, from the level of our most intimate relationships to the level of international politics. There is a saying that if one wants peace in the world then one must have peace in the home, but this must be held alongside another saying that there is more to peace than the absence of war. Peace and justice go hand in hand, and they encompass every dimension of our lives – sex, politics, religion and culture. There is no point in hungering after a world of peace if our most intimate relationships are still disrupted by violence and conflict. A violent sexual relationship breeds violent children, and violent children breed violent societies. I am writing this as the tragic aftermath of the James Bulger case continues to unfold, when the two abused and neglected children who murdered the two-year-old have now been released under threat of vigilante attacks and mob violence. Two small domestic realms of misery and poverty have thus exploded to create shock waves of violence that have rippled out and out through society. The task of weaving together a better world begins in those areas where violence first seeded itself in human relationships – in the restoration of dignity and equality to sexual love, and in the healing of the fratricidal envy that patriarchy breeds among the sons of God and men.

This is not a Utopian vision. We all know firsthand the conflict between our longing for harmonious and loving lives and the realities of living together as lovers, spouses, families, communities and nations. How many of us as mothers know the wrenching guilt of resolving to be more patient, more attentive, more engaged, only to find ourselves exploding at our children because we have bottled up too much in the effort to live out the maternal ideals society and the Church put upon us?

We cannot fake peace. It has to begin from deep within, as a transformation of self, which is the work of a lifetime. Perhaps it really is only the saints who finally show us what the achievement of peace looks like – peace with ourselves, peace with God, peace with the world. This ongoing work of peace requires a leap of faith that can carry us beyond all the failures we experience and engender among us. It requires a continual attitude of repentance and forgiveness, which makes us open and vulnerable to the sorrow and healing of broken relationships. Etty Hillesum, a secular Dutch Jew who died in Auschwitz, imagines what she wishes she could say to a grieving Jewish mother whose son was killed by the Nazis:

> Ought we not, from time to time, to open ourselves up to cosmic sadness? ... Give your sorrow all the space and shelter in yourself that is its due, for if everyone bears his grief honestly and courageously, the sorrow that now fills the world will abate. But if you do not clear a decent shelter for your sorrow, and instead reserve most of the space inside you for hatred and thoughts of revenge – from which new sorrows will be born for others – then sorrow will never cease in this world and will multiply. And if you have given sorrow the space its gentle origins demand, then you may truly say: life is beautiful and so rich. So beautiful and so rich that it makes you want to believe in God.[23]

Our world today gives cause for 'cosmic sadness', a sadness that is intimately bound up in the failure of Christian history and in the realization that the most destructive and militaristic nations in the world are those that have been most shaped by the Christian tradition. But Hillesum also suggests that sorrow is in itself an antidote to violence, and a step towards the healing we need to appreciate anew the beauty of the world and God.

Sorrow also allows us to accommodate failure without fury or denial. As human beings, we know that there are wounds that will not heal, betrayals that cannot be forgiven, injustices that are not set right. Our dream of salvation and wholeness is played out in Eve's world, and with her we suffer the consequences of our own weaknesses and temptations, and the anguish of our children's inheritance of sin.

Yet as mothers of the living, we women hold the future in our hands, and all over the world a small but significant minority of women is refusing to collude in the structures of violence. It is becoming more and more difficult to mask the wounded love of wives and mothers beneath the flags and banners of men's victories. The women of Greenham Common remain a potent symbol of what is possible when women dare to say 'no' to the powers of militarism and violence. They represent what Jean Bethke Elshtain calls the 'potentia', the subversive potency of women's power, which has the capacity to disrupt and undermine the 'potestas' of masculine power, which rules the world. She writes, 'Women, from a double position that straddles powerlessness and power, are in a powerful position to insist with Albert Camus that one must never avert one's eyes from the suffering of children and, seeing that suffering one is required to act.'[24]

Tapping into this source of women's power entails what feminists call 'empowerment'. It is the discovery within oneself of a source of strength and solidarity that allows one to work with others, not in competition and conflict but in co-operation and harmony. We do not always succeed, and women no less than men are vulnerable to the forces of envy and aggression that can insinuate themselves with such destructive subtlety into our bonds of friendship and love. But throughout the world today, there is a growing network of women working across boundaries of religion, class, race and nation to say 'no' to what diminishes and brutalizes the children of the human family and 'yes' to what brings life, flourishing and wholeness to ourselves and the garden of creation. Eve's daughters are speaking today. Can her sons pause in their murderous games for long enough to listen?

The Colosseum broods in the heart of Rome, pregnant with symbolic meanings. It has been neither torn down nor restored, and today its Christian symbols and ceremonies juxtapose themselves in a strange and awkward relationship to its imperial past. Like the Church herself, the Colosseum continues to represent both the futility and the seduction of violence. Symbol of a timeless empire and its emperors, it warns against such hubristic visions. Focal point of so much romantic poetry and art, it colludes in the romanticization of violence and the glorification of empire. Ruined but beautiful, it speaks of the ways in which perhaps our human imagination unavoidably situates us in that place of encounter between love and violence, sex and death, murder and martyrdom, hope and desolation.

In this night of broken symbols, we yearn for new visions and new dreams. All the ideologies we have tried, all the failed visions we have pursued so far in history, have been formulated and implemented by men. Today, for the first time, it is women rather than men who are beginning to imagine tomorrow's world. Women's voices are telling new stories, herstories, which remind us that history is only one version of the truth, only one way of seeing the world.

But even so, we should be wary of a Utopianism that forgets the humility and attentiveness needed to change the world from the inside out, from the depths of the human heart where all violence starts, to the structures and institutions of the global order. In recent years a number of Christian thinkers such as John Milbank and James Alison have argued that political liberation movements, including liberation theology, cannot help but emulate the violence they seek to overcome. The Brazilian feminist theologian Ivone Gebara suggests that

The liberator God, in spite of the attractiveness of the concept, sometimes seems as dangerous as the God of reason, who governs the world from a throne of glory. In practice this image of God as liberator excludes women as much as does the image of God as 'the Other', in so far as women continue to be the pietàs of war games, accepting on their knees the murdered bodies of husbands, lovers, brothers, sisters, children, parents.[25]

The French philosopher and cultural theorist Michel Foucault argues that power is woven into all our relationships, so that it is never possible to escape its capacity to oppress and distort our social interactions. At best, we can only subvert and negotiate power relations in order to seek a space of freedom within them.[26]

But against these necessary cautions it is also important to remember that Christianity has as its core symbols the most radical possible affirmations of the power of love manifest in powerlessness and vulnerability, in the infant God in the manger and the dying God on the cross. Jon Sobrino, writing in the aftermath of the murder of his Jesuit colleagues, his housekeeper and her daughter at the University of El Salvador, describes what this powerlessness amounts to:

> The cross reveals, not power, but impotence. God does not triumph on the cross over the power of evil, but succumbs to it.... The idea that in the battle of the gods the true God could lose and through that defeat prove himself the true God requires us to rethink his transcendence. Part of God's greatness is his making himself small. And, paradoxically, in this plan of his taking on what is small God makes himself a greater mystery, a new and greater transcendence, than the stammered definitions of human beings.[27]

Faced with the violent gods of the social order and the imperial status quo – Roman, Christian or secular – the God of Christ cannot but be defeated in the eyes of the world. Many would argue that women must use the language of the cross with care, for too often in the past the suffering, self-giving victimhood of Christ has been projected onto women, while his divine power and victory have been appropriated by men. It is a delicate task to combine solidarity and resistance with compassion and care, to gently call the future into being with a wisdom that can tell the difference between suffering that must be endured and suffering that must be resisted, the liberating poverty of a simple life and the crushing poverty experienced through war, violence and injustice.

With so many urgent tasks confronting us, should we do something, or should we perhaps actively commit ourselves to doing nothing? Can we afford the luxury of a fallow era: an era when we reimagine our stories of being, becoming and belonging, an era when we become daydreamers and visionaries instead of empire builders and masters of the world? Maybe that is what we need more than anything else, a long day of rest, a Sabbath when we and the world might renew our resources, replenish our storerooms of wisdom and faith, and listen to voices that speak of promised beginnings.

So come with me now away from the roar of traffic on Mussolini's highways, away from the ruined majesty of the Colosseum, through the ancient lanes and alleyways of the city, to explore 'the road less travelled'. We can try to imagine different paths Christianity might have taken, paths the Church might still take in her quest to build God's city on earth.

Notes

1. John Ferguson, *War and Peace in the World's Religions* (London: Sheldon Press, 1977), p. 122.
2. See Thomas Weidemann, 'Emperors, Gladiators and Christians', in *Omnibus*, 22 (September 1991), pp. 26–8, reproduced in The Open University, *An Introduction to the Humanities, Resource Book 1* (Milton Keynes: The Open University, 1999): pp. 101–7.
3. See René Girard, *The Girard Reader*, ed. James G. Williams (New York: Crossroad Herder, 1996); Girard, *Things Hidden Since the Foundation of the World*, trans. Stephen Bann and Michael Metteer (London: The Athlone Press, 1987).

4. Cf. John Pearson, *Arena: The Story of The Colosseum* (London: Thames and Hudson, 1973), Chapter 10.

5. Julia Kristeva, 'Stabat Mater', in *Tales of Love*, trans. Leon S. Roudiez (New York: Columbia University Press, 1987): p. 241.

6. Jonathan Magonet, *A Rabbi's Bible* (London: SCM Press, 1991), p. 114.

7. Ibid., p. 122.

8. Tikva Frymer-Kensky, *In the Wake of the Goddesses: Women, Culture and the Biblical Transformation of Pagan Myth* (New York: Fawcett Columbine, 1992), p. 109.

9. Honnor Morton, *From a Nurse's Note-book (1899)*, quoted in Martha Vicinus, *Independent Women: Work and Community for Single Women, 1850–1920* (Chicago, IL: University of Chicago Press, 1988).

10. See Girard, *Things Hidden*, p. 39.

11. Ibid., pp. 180–223.

12. Gerard W. Hughes, *God of Surprises* (London: Darton, Longman & Todd, 1987), p. 35.

13. Thérèse of Lisieux, *The Story of a Soul*, p. 111.

14. 'Epistle to Diogenetus', in J. Stevenson, *A New Eusebius: Documents Illustrating the History of the Church to AD 337*, new edn, rev. W. H. C. Frend (London: SPCK, 1987): pp. 55–6.

15. Ferguson, *War and Peace*, p. 103.

16. Elaine Pagels, *Adam, Eve and the Serpent* (London: Weidenfeld & Nicolson, 1988), p. xxv.

17. Ibid., p. xxvi.

18. Clement of Alexandria, *Exhortation to the Heathen, II* (Ante-Nicene Fathers, Vol. 3), pp. 99–100, quoted in Timothy George, 'A Radically Christian Witness for Peace' in Haim Gordon and Leonard Grob (eds), *Education for Peace: Testimonies from World Religions* (Maryknoll, NY: Orbis, 1987): pp. 62–76, p. 67.

19. See Roger Ruston, *War of Religions, Religion of War* (Manchester: Blackfriars Publications, 1993).

20. See George, 'A Radically Christian Witness', p. 69.

21. See Girard, *Things Hidden*, pp. 260–2.

22. Quoted in Jeanne Vickers, *Women and War* (London and New Jersey: Zed Books, 1993), p. 36.

23. Etty Hillesum, *An Interrupted Life: The Diaries, 1941–1943 and Letters from Westerbork*, trans. Arnold J. Pomerans (New York: Henry Holt, 1996), p. 96.

24. Jean Bethke Elshtain, 'The Power and Powerlessness of Women', in Gisela Bock and Susan James (eds), *Beyond Equality and Difference: Citizenship, Feminist Politics and Female Subjectivity* (London and New York: Routledge, 1992): pp. 110–25, p. 122.

25. Ivone Gebara, 'The Face of Transcendence as a Challenge to the Reading of the Bible in Latin America', in Elisabeth Schüssler Fiorenza (ed.), *Searching the Scriptures: A Feminist Introduction* (London: SCM Press, 1993): pp. 172–86, p. 175.

26. See Michel Foucault, *The History of Sexuality, Volume 1 – An Introduction* (London: Penguin, 1990).

27. Jon Sobrino, *Jesus the Liberator*, trans. Paul Burns and Francis McDonagh (Tunbridge Wells: Burns & Oates, 1994), pp. 248–9.

St Anne and the Virgin Mary, Lorenzo Toni, The Pantheon

3

Baptizing Eve:
The Pantheon

Christian and pagan encounters

If the Colosseum makes a bold and unambiguous statement about
the violence as well as the genius of imperial Rome, the Pantheon
is a more subtle and complex artefact. Compared to the Colosseum, it suggests a sense of continuity and preservation. While
the Colosseum was allowed to fall into a state of disrepair, the
Pantheon seems to have made a more natural transition from
pagan temple to Christian church. Its magnificent dome still
attests to the architectural genius of Rome, while its dedication
to the Virgin Mary since the seventh century makes a statement
about the enduring impact of the Catholic faith.

The Colosseum invites reflection on the relationship between
male power, violence and imperialism in Christian history, but
the Pantheon might allow for a more creative and speculative
interpretation, based not on history itself but on what might have
been and might yet come to be. It hints at an alternative scenario,
one that has been played out on the margins of the imperial
Church, suggesting perhaps another, different way of living and
loving in the name of Christ.

As its name suggests, the Pantheon was first built as a temple
to the Roman gods, by the emperor Agrippa between 27 and 25
BC, and after being destroyed by fire it was rebuilt by Hadrian

between AD 120 and 125. Its design seems to communicate a quest for the universality and harmony of the divine. The vast dome is open to the heavens and forms a perfect semi-sphere which would be completed if it extended down to touch the floor. The rotunda's interior niches might once have held statues of the planetary deities – Mercury, Mars, Venus, Jupiter, the Moon, the Sun and Saturn – who together controlled the time and space of the cosmos. Although rebuilt by Hadrian, the façade bears the original dedication to Agrippa, a self-effacing gesture on Hadrian's part that increases the enigmatic quality of the building, so that it represents more than just another imperial vanity.

Early in the seventh century, when Rome had dwindled into neglect, the Byzantine Emperor Phocas gave the Pantheon to Pope Boniface IV, who consecrated it to St Mary of All Martyrs in May 609 or 610. The feast of All Saints in the Western Church is traced back to that occasion, although it originated earlier in the Eastern Church, where it is still celebrated on the first Sunday after Pentecost. In the ninth century Pope Gregory IV changed the date of the feast to 1 November, possibly in an attempt to christianize pagan festivals of the dead, which took place at that time of year. Long before the arrival of Christianity in Britain, the Celts had been celebrating the festival of Samhain, Lord of the Dead, on the night between 31 October and 1 November. Some scholars argue that there is a close connection between All Saints and Samhain.

The Pantheon of the Roman gods today stands as a monument to the pantheon of the Christian saints, presided over by the majestic presence of the Virgin Mary and inviting renewed reflection on the relationship between paganism and Christianity. Does Catholicism represent the destruction or the redemption of pagan religion? If Christ is the redeemer of the cosmos in whom all things are reconciled and made new, then his saving grace should encompass every dream of heaven, every experience of the divine, suffusing all that is with the peace and love of God so that it becomes transformed in the incarnation. But paganism evokes some of the deepest and darkest terrors of the Christian mind, representing those dimensions of life that the men of the Church have tried to exclude from the story of salvation – female sexuality, goddess worship, priestesses, Eve and the flesh. These haunt the theological imagination and threaten to unravel its tidy arguments and justifications. To see the Pantheon through the eyes of Eve is to ask disturbing questions about the redemption of the female body, the divinization of woman made in the image of God, and the inclusion of woman *qua* woman in the story of salvation. What does the Virgin Mary represent in that context? Like the cross in the Colosseum, she is an ambiguous symbol, open to different interpretations.

Mary, Eve and the goddess

By the time of the Pantheon's dedication, Mary had taken on the role of a Byzantine empress, a figure both of popular devotion and imperial power. Some would argue that she had become the goddess of the Christian religion, taking the place of the *Magna Mater*, the Great Mother of the pagan cults. To quote Stephen Benko, 'Mariology does not simply resemble pagan customs and ideas ... it is paganism baptized, pure and simple.'[1]

But from a woman's point of view, this argument is at best only partly true. The cult of Mary has given rise to feminized forms of spirituality and worship which might indeed make her something of a goddess figure for women as well as men, but these have largely been excluded from the official doctrines and liturgies of the Church. There is an uneasy relationship between popular Marian devotions and the institutional Church, presided over by an exclusively male hierarchy. If Mariology is paganism baptized, then one has to ask whether it represents the baptism of

the pagan matriarchal cults with their mother–daughter figures
and their fertility rituals, or the baptism of patriarchal paganism
with its oedipal father-gods and their attendant consorts.

As will be seen, the answer is both, for if official Catholicism
bears many of the marks of pagan patriarchy, the ancient goddesses and their female devotees still whisper and beckon in the
cult of Mary. There have been times when the mother–daughter
relationship and the earth's fertility have been central to Marian
iconography and devotion: times when Catholic Christianity
might have gone beyond either patriarchy or matriarchy to
become a body of human beings truly reconciled and redeemed
in the peace of Christ. The symbols and values of matriarchal
religion are still woven into Catholic sacramentality, stripped of
their maternal feminine potency and rendered inaccessible to
female priests and celebrants, but ripe for regeneration and
rehabitation by the bodies of living, worshipping women.

This raises the question: to what extent do the public rituals of
Catholicism express the gendered nature of human life, so that
women as well as men might participate in worship as bodily
creatures made in the image of God and divinized in Christ? In
asking this question, it is necessary to explore in more detail what
might be meant by masculine and feminine forms of religion. It
is also important to consider the ways in which Eve, far from
being a peripheral or insignificant figure in the formation of
Christian identity and orthodoxy, has been the dark and threatening other who has defined the Church by marking the boundaries of redemption. In Christian culture, Mary has represented
the redeemed creature and Eve has represented the unredeemed
other – the sexual woman, pagan goddess and priestess who have
never yet been baptized by Christianity.

But to study writings on Eve in the Early Church is to discover
a more nuanced picture than this, for Eve is not simply the polar
opposite of Mary. Rather, she is part of a prismatic image of

salvation in which negative and dualistic imagery is subverted through a more intricate understanding of the relationship and indeed the interdependency between the two women. Sometimes they even seem to represent one and the same individual in her aspects of sin and grace, fallenness and redemption. Some patristic interpretations of the Magnificat describe it as Eve's hymn of redemption. She is the lowly handmaid who is exalted in Mary. A fifth-century Syrian bishop, Severian, wrote,

> Hear what the Virgin herself in prophecy says. 'Blessed be the Lord God of Israel, because He has regarded the humility of His handmaid: for from henceforth all generations shall call me blessed.' In order thus to show that she bears the person of Eve: Me, she says, until now despised, henceforth shall all generations call me Blessed.[2]

According to this interpretation, Eve and Mary together represent the redemption of woman, for it is only by knowing what it means to be fallen that we can understand what it means to be redeemed. It is as if, in order to represent Mary, the Early Church had to construct her opposite out of the shadowy and relatively insignificant figure of the biblical Eve. In some patristic writings, Eve is the face of women's sorrow while Mary is the joyful face of women's salvation. Mary is the eschatological woman of the new creation, whereas Eve is Everywoman, representing both the promise of fulfilment and the reality of suffering.

Justin and Irenaeus, writing in the second century, were the first to develop an elaborate typology of Mary and Eve, in which Mary as the New Eve is the feminine equivalent to Christ as the New Adam. Thus the incarnation came to be interpreted as a creation narrative, in which Mary is both the virgin earth of Paradise from which the second Adam is born and the woman companion to the first man of the new creation. The purpose of this typology was threefold: it enabled Christians to see the coming of Christ foreshadowed in the events and characters of the Old Testament (an interpretation which today causes controversy among those who respect the integrity of the Hebrew Scriptures in the context of Judaism); it allowed for a gendered understanding of salvation, so that the male and female bodies were both redeemed in the persons of Mary and Christ; and it embodied Christ in the story of the world from the beginning, so that there was no aspect of creation not incorporated within the incarnation. By tracing Mary's genealogy back to Eve, Irenaeus and those who followed him situated the life of Christ in the midst of the time and space of the world's existence. Thus while Mary's virginity was a theological symbol, which attested to the divine nature of Christ and the redemptive intervention of God in history, her motherhood was an anthropological symbol, which safeguarded the human nature of Christ, protected the continuity of the human story, and affirmed the tangible, material reality of the incarnate God.

But if the relationship between Mary and Eve communicated theological insights about the nature of redemption and the interpretation of the Bible to the first Christians, it was also used to situate women in relation to the Church and to the pagan cults and Gnostic sects. Several patristic writings make an explicit connection between Eve and the women in the mystery cults in which the serpent was a phallic fertility symbol. There is a symbolic association between women who model themselves on Mary by becoming Christians and women who model themselves on Eve by remaining in the cults. Some feminists would see this as evidence that, from the beginning, Christianity was a patriarchal religion, which set out to destroy woman-centred religions and the challenge they posed to its masculine authority structures. While there may be some truth in this, it is a reductive interpretation, which fails to do justice to the complex motives and beliefs of the Early Church.

A number of scholars have argued that these cults were not thriving women's religions of peace, harmony and sexual self-expression that were annihilated by the patriarchal Church. They were in themselves patriarchal religions in which women's power was limited and their freedom often curtailed. For example, Robin Lane Fox suggests that the vestal virgins were part of the temple cult of imperial Rome, and sometimes this involved being taken into captivity as children.[3] However idyllic the Elysian mysteries might once have been in the ancient mists of time, by the first centuries of the Christian era they had degenerated into violent and abusive rituals. Even allowing for Christian polemic, it is clear that the main objection to the cults was that they were degrading for those who participated in them. Augustine, recalling rituals he had witnessed as a young man, asks what kind of deities would demand such debasement of their followers, and bemoans the lack of maternal respect evident in the abusive worship of the Mother Goddess.[4] Another fourth-century Christian writer with probable experience of the cult of Mithraism, Firmicus Maternicus, is explicit in identifying Eve with the women in the cults, which he condemns for their brutalization of poor and vulnerable people.[5]

From this point of view, Mary represents the woman who is obedient not to the pagan gods and goddesses but to the God of Israel incarnate in Christ, who confers dignity and freedom upon those who worship him. The comparison between Mary and Eve was therefore played out in the actual religious experiences of women, and among other things it was possibly an attempt to convince women that the path to liberation lay in abandoning the enslavement of the cults, in order to follow the example of Mary rather than Eve. As the discussion of Pagels' work in the last chapter showed, freedom was seen as the most important quality of the Christian life in the first centuries, and for women as well as men Christ offered freedom from the tyranny of the pagan divinities.

Yet at the same time there was probably considerable movement between the Church and the cults. Fox suggests that women converts to Christianity were often highly independent characters who did not willingly submit to the moralizing of the Church's male leaders.[6] The idea of lifelong virginity was a Christian innovation that might have been easier to sustain in theory than in practice. The vestal virgins were not literally virgins because they practised cultic sex. Women converts to Christianity were sometimes attracted back by the more relaxed sexual attitudes of the cults, and patristic fulminations against the weakness of women and the temptation of Eve might be directed against such women. So the relationship between Eve and Mary in the first four centuries describes a complex and fluid social reality, while at the same time setting in place a Christian symbolics of good and bad womanhood that would endure long after the cults had disappeared.

The defeat of the goddess

Developments in the fifth century led to several decisive shifts in the Church that implicitly affected the positioning of Eve. First, Christian patriarchy was secured by the conversion of Rome. In the newly institutionalized Roman Church, women were assigned to positions of subordination and inferiority in a more decisive way than in the first four centuries. Second, the pagan cults had been destroyed and Christian interpretations had been superimposed on the earlier pagan deities. Images of Christ from that time often bear a striking resemblance to Apollo, and those of Mary resemble some of the pagan goddesses, such as the Egyptian

Isis and her son Osiris. The Christian dedication of the Pantheon belongs within a widespread movement in which temples and shrines were consecrated to Mary. Thus the living and perhaps ambivalent reality of pagan women's religions and their symbols of divine femininity were overlaid with an idealized form of Christian womanhood, stripped of any specific woman-centred cult or priesthood. Third, Christianity was becoming more dualistic, both in its attitude towards the body and sexuality and in its theological vision. Asceticism was taking the place of martyrdom as the way of making the body suffer for Christ, and ideas of the relationship between God and humankind were beginning to focus more on distance than on intimacy, more on the awesome power of God than on the reconciling love of the incarnation. Jürgen Moltmann suggests that the 'Romanisation of the image of God ... involved transferring the Roman *patria potestas* to God.'[7]

By the end of the fifth century paganism had been driven far beneath the surface of the Christian faith, although many of its beliefs and practices continued to thrive in the folk religions that have always existed on the margins of Catholic culture. Christians would again encounter those they called 'pagan' in the era of missionary expansionism, but in the intervening centuries the idea of the pagan provided a fertile breeding ground for all the embryonic fantasies and fears of the Early Church. Geoffrey Ashe describes the 'utter revulsion'[8] with which the first Christians rejected paganism, and that revulsion has endured even though the Church has eradicated any overt traces of paganism from its domain.

But no matter how degenerate the cults, it is hard to account for the degree of hostility that they inspired among early Christians. It is unlikely that even at their most orgiastic they could rival the violence of the imperial cult focused on public places such as the Colosseum, and yet the games never excited the Christian imagination to the extent that the cults did. If Cain spilled his brother's blood again and again in the sands of the arena, it was Eve's sexuality, not the violence of her son, that ultimately defined the Christian understanding of sin.

Sexual annihilation

While Roman Christianity achieved some degree of tolerance with regard to imperial violence, it set its face ferociously against pagan religion with its women priestesses and adherents. Today, some people are beginning to count the cost of that rejection. Lynn White traces the beginnings of the environmental crisis back to the early Christian desacralization of nature, when sacred trees were felled and shrines destroyed as a protest against pantheism.[9] There is evidence that on at least one occasion this destructive impulse extended to the murder of a renowned pagan woman. In 415 a Christian mob set upon the Alexandrian philosopher Hypatia and killed her in the most brutal way, by carrying her into a church, stripping her, and scraping the flesh from her bones with oyster shells. At the time this might have been an isolated incident, but between the fifteenth and eighteenth centuries hundreds of thousands of women were burned at the stake or drowned as witches. We know very few of the names of those who died, such as Joan of Arc and Marguerite Porète, but during those centuries Christian men of power annihilated some of the Western world's brightest and most outstanding women – women of independence and courage who would rather face the most terrible death than conform to the demands of an authoritarian male hierarchy.

But why has Christianity focused so much of its fury and blame on women in general and on female sexuality in particular? There is nothing in the Gospels, and little in the Pauline letters, to account for the physical and intellectual tyranny against women that is an ongoing reality of the Catholic faith. On issues ranging from the female priesthood to the feminization of language about God and the ecclesiastical control of women's fertility, there is something deeply problematic about the ways in which Catholic men in positions of authority understand the religious and social significance of the female body. What are they afraid of?

Partly, the answer might lie in Girard's theory that sex serves as a mask for violence. Girard argues that the imperative to conceal the scapegoating mechanism means that violence is often justified through attributing some form of sexual transgression to the victim, whose persecution then masquerades as a form of justice rather than random victimization.[10] Thinking of this in the context of Christianity's tolerance of violence and its rejection of sex, one could argue that men's inability to acknowledge their implication in Cain's act of violence means that they project blame on to Eve's sexuality instead. Rather than recognizing Cain's murder of Abel as the original sin, Christianity has implied that Cain murdered Abel because he was the victim of his mother's original sin of seduction. Thus for two millennia the theological imagination has focused not on the problem of Cain's violence as the greatest challenge to Christian love but on the problem of Eve's sexuality. This invites further reflection from the point of view of psychoanalysis, because it brings into question the ways in which the maternal as well as the sexual female body might be perceived as a threat to masculine identity and control.

Psychoanalysis in its various forms points to the ambiguity that marks the original maternal relationship. The mother is an all-powerful figure who represents both life and death, nurture and deprivation. The young child experiences extremes of love and hate, tenderness and fury, in its relationship with her. In cultures that still have feminine deities, such as Mahayana Buddhism and Hinduism, and in ancient religious mythologies, mother-goddesses are ferocious as well as tender, holding the power of both life and death.

Julia Kristeva describes the ambivalence of the maternal relationship in terms of love and abjection.[11] The realm of the unconscious associated with the mother is the source of an insatiable, inexpressible yearning for union and love, but it is also the source of an inconsolable, unspeakable dread of death and annihilation. The maternal body consumes as well as nurtures, destroys life as well as creating it. In the process of socialization we learn to repress these powerful positive and negative feelings associated with the mother, but they do not go away. They become part of our psychological make-up, the dimension of the unconscious, which has the power to disturb and disrupt the processes of conscious thought and behaviour.

In tracing the origins of this unconscious maternal anxiety, Kristeva argues that Western culture is the result of a long developmental process, which begins with the purity laws of the Old Testament, when the people of Israel first felt called to set themselves apart for God by distancing themselves from the maternal pagan cults.[12] The Levitical codes mark out the boundaries of purity and impurity, and that which is deemed polluting is closely associated with the maternal body and also with the limits of identity, where bodily secretions blur the boundaries of the physical self. Blood, milk, semen, menstruating and postnatal women, and ultimately the corpse itself are reminders of the defiling potency of the maternal body with its threat of annihilation and loss of distinction. Identity depends upon separation from the mother. The people of Israel became a people of the law set apart by God, deriving their identity from an ethical rather than a carnal relationship to their God and from a patriarchal rather than a matriarchal divinity.

Scholars like Baring and Cashford see this process of separation and rejection being played out around the figure of Eve in the story of Genesis. She is the Great Mother, the goddess who is identified with the serpent and with the tree of knowledge as symbols of fertility and wisdom. But in the confrontation in Genesis, the patriarchal God of monotheism triumphs over the goddess, wresting from her the power of life and leaving her unambiguously identified with death. To quote John Philips: 'The history of Eve begins with the appearance of Yahweh in the place of the Mother of All the Living. This shift of power marks a fundamental change in the relationship between humanity and God, the world and God, the world and humanity, and men and women.'[13]

Kristeva argues that by breaching the Levitical codes, Christ achieved a reconciliation between ethical monotheism and the maternal cults.[14] He was a Jew who touched bleeding women and lepers, who violated the Sabbath law, and who identified the person of God with the ultimate source of pollution – the corpse on the cross. In his teaching, he also reversed the order of pollution – henceforth, defilement would come from the inside, not from the outside, and it was a product of language rather than of material substances: 'What goes into the mouth does not make a man unclean; it is what comes out of the mouth that makes him unclean' (Matthew 15:10).

Kristeva suggests that Christ alone achieved reconciliation between the body and the word, harmoniously integrating the idea of the abject or the polluting flesh with the language of the spiritual, so that the flesh itself acquired a transcendent, spiritualized quality. But Christianity failed to sustain this sense of reconciling integration between the body and language. Rather, it retained a sense of guilt associated with the maternal body and pollution and called it sin. Thus transgression and the breaching of the Levitical taboos were translated into a new form of subjectivity, produced by Christian consciousness, in which the struggle between sin and grace, the body of the mother and the law of the father, has become a psychological phenomenon expressed in language, rather than a religious phenomenon expressed in purity laws. Instead of a world marked out by physical boundaries of the sacred and profane, the pure and the impure, the Christian psyche itself became the domain where these boundaries operate. Thus in the formation of Western consciousness, with its Judaeo-Christian inheritance, psychoanalysis reveals to us an inner life structured around a conscious, symbolic order associated with the Father's law, and a repressed unconscious seething with the images, desires and fears associated with the forbidden maternal body.

Kristeva argues that Catholic Christianity sublimates rather than represses this maternal aspect. The cult of the Virgin allows for its limited and controlled expression, although in a spiritualized form, so that the language of Marian devotion lacks any real association with the functions of the female flesh. It is post-Catholic culture, deprived of any public maternal symbolism, which according to Kristeva lacks a language and a form of expression for the mother. She suggests that modern secular culture stands in urgent need of a new ethics, an 'herethics',[15] in which the body and its associations with birth, death and the maternal flesh is incorporated into rather than excluded from language and ethics. This would entail recognizing and accepting ourselves, not as the autonomous masculine subject of post-Enlightenment philosophy and culture, but as divided beings, estranged from ourselves, neither masculine nor feminine but always in the process of becoming in the haunted, desiring space between abjection and love.

It would be a mistake to take this hypothesis too literally, since there is an infinite complexity to gender relations and to the relationship between the body and language in Christian culture. However, Kristeva does invite us to reflect upon latent associations between the historical reality of the Christian encounter with paganism, the psychological identification of Eve with the idea of sin and its associations with the sexual, maternal body, and the elevation of Mary to a transcendent and asexual maternal ideal who is 'full of grace' because her capacity to represent the sexual, bleeding, birthing, nurturing and devouring mother has been projected onto Eve. Therefore Catholic Christianity, like the goddess religions, has potentially not one but two forms of goddess – the good mother and the bad mother, the compassionate mother and the deadly mother, the nurturing mother and the devouring mother. And for two thousand years the female body has borne the wounds of this split because, with its sublime vision of reconciliation between word and flesh, God and creation, male and female, Christianity has never sustained the reconciliation between Eve and Mary that forms part of its earliest theology of salvation.

Faced with the enormous cultural and religious task of healing this wound inflicted by a dualistic and disincarnate theology of woman, how might modern Catholic feminists create the imaginative beginnings of a new religious culture? This would be based not on masculine domination and feminine subordination but on a gendered understanding of the story of redemption played out in an holistic and liberating liturgical environment.

Feminizing religion

What would a woman-centred religion be like? For many religious feminists, Christian and non-Christian alike, the quest for a maternal feminine symbolics entails the creative reclamation and reinvention of the myths, rituals and ideas associated with the goddess figures of the pre-Christian world. For Christian feminists, this means embracing rather than rejecting some of the values and practices associated with the pagan goddesses. What did these figures symbolize, and do they represent an alternative to the sacrificial violence of masculine religion? In responding to such questions, feminists are less concerned with historical facts than with mythical possibilities. It is almost impossible to ascertain to what extent the ancient goddess religions might have represented genuine alternatives to patriarchal religion, and feminists have been criticized for their romanticized and ahistorical view of these cults. However, a more nuanced approach recognizes that the construction of different religious narratives is a literary rather than an historical venture, entailing as it does a quest for new symbolic meanings rather than old historic truths.

The figures of Demeter and Kore/Persephone are often referred to as resources for a feminist critique and reclamation of religious mythology. Symbolically, if not historically, they evoke a time of transition in Western religious consciousness, from matriarchal to patriarchal divinities and cults. Demeter is the fertility goddess of corn and fruit. Her daughter, Persephone (also known as Kore), is abducted by Pluto, God of the Underworld, and Demeter's grief as she searches for her lost daughter causes the crops to fail and winter to descend on the earth. Finally, a bargain is struck whereby Persephone is permitted to spend six months of every year above ground with her mother, on condition that she spends six months in the Underworld with her husband. The earth flourishes during the times when mother and daughter are reconciled, and it becomes barren during the months of their separation.

The myth suggests an intimate relationship between mother–daughter love, the seasons and the earth's fecundity. But it also describes the aggressive intrusion of masculine deities, so that the kidnap and rape of Persephone becomes a metaphor for the ways in which patriarchal cultures and religions exercise a regime of possession and violence, which destroys bonds between women and afflicts the fertility and harmony of nature. For feminists such as Irigaray, the positive symbolization of the mother–daughter relationship and the restoration of maternal genealogies is a necessary counterbalance to the dominance of the father–son relationship and paternal genealogies in Western religion and culture.[16]

So where might Christian women turn to if they want to piece together a religious narrative in which mothers and daughters feature as bearers of the divine, equal to but different from fathers and sons, and in which fertility and nature are celebrated as manifestations of God? Is it possible to remain faithful to the Catholic tradition, while also experimenting and engaging with the insights of the feminist goddess movements? And what resources does the Marian tradition offer for this task of religious reconstruction and reclamation?

Setting aside for now the theological difficulties inherent in claiming goddess status for Mary, in her present form she could only be a goddess in captivity to patriarchy. Radical feminists such as Mary Daly and Luce Irigaray see her as emblematic of the 'fembots' (Daly) or 'regulation Athenae' (Irigaray) who collude in the patriarchal status quo by playing out the roles of dutiful and beautiful wives, mothers, daughters and mistresses. For many women, Mary is a mother who disempowers her daughters and subjects them to the tyranny of the Father's law through the negation of their sexuality and the denial of any sense of self-worth and autonomy. Moreover, while goddesses such as Demeter and Persephone symbolize loving relationships between women, in modern Catholicism Mary is 'alone of all her sex', while all other women are implicitly identified with Eve. Although millions of men and women in every age and culture have found Mary a source of consolation and celebration, for many others she is an anachronistic and oppressive figure who bears down upon women with the accumulated weight of two thousand years of masculine fantasies, projections and fears. The modern Marian tradition seems to offer few resources for the creation of a maternal feminine religious paradigm such as that envisaged by some feminists. Mary towers in judgement and condemnation over Eve and her sisters, her virginal purity and asexual motherhood serving as a reminder that an ordinary woman's body would be a polluting and unworthy receptacle for the Son of God.

But however problematic the Virgin Mary might be for women today, the sentimental and impoverished stereotypes of modern art and devotion fail to do justice to the rich complexity of the Marian tradition. Undoubtedly, with the conversion of Rome, Mary too was incorporated into a more rigidly hierarchical and patriarchal system than had been the case before, and devotion to Mary, Queen of Peace, has done little to curb the violence of her devotees. Nicholas Perry and Loreto Echeverría have written a highly critical study, *Under the Heel of Mary*,[17] showing the extent to which Mary has been used as a bulwark to defend the papacy and advance the power of the Church. She has ridden into battle on the banners of crusaders and conquistadors, she is associated with medieval miracle stories that reflect Christian hatred of the Jews, and in the modern Church her image is appropriated by those who seek power over women's bodies through the legal and moral control of reproduction and sexuality. From the perspective offered by Perry and Echeverría, the evidence against Mary is overwhelmingly negative. For other critics like Marina Warner, she is an anachronism who might once have served a useful cultural function but who is no longer relevant to the modern world.[18] But for women who seek to combine fidelity to the Catholic tradition with feminist religious consciousness, I believe that the Marian tradition offers a wealth of images, symbols, values and ideas that provide a rich resource for the transformation and renewal of Christianity.

Because Mary is such a powerful figure in the Catholic imagination – invested as she is with the potent but repressed undercurrents of the maternal dimension of Western culture with its dreams and nightmares, longings and terrors – feminists will not easily rescue her from the clutches of men of power and their dutiful handmaids. Nevertheless, while it is important not to underestimate the extent to which Mary is enmeshed in the Church's deepest structures of control, this is still only part of the story. For there are different ways of understanding Mary, and the long traditions surrounding her invite reappraisal for those who seek maternal feminine images of love and redemption in Christ.

I have already referred to the movement between the cults and the Church among early women converts to Christianity, but this is part of a complex and forgotten tapestry of women's religious worlds in the first centuries of the Christian era. Any attempt to reimagine those worlds must necessarily involve a great deal of speculation and hypothesis, but even so there are tantalizing glimmers of ideas and practices which invite creative interpretation.

Gendered rites

Ashe's study of Marian devotion in the first three centuries leads him to speculate that there might have been a women's movement focused on Mary, parallel to but possibly operating independently of the male-led church. He describes this as 'a dissident body which also traced its inspiration to the gospel events, but paid its chief homage to the Virgin, as Queen of Heaven and (in effect) a form of the Goddess; and it was composed mainly of women'.[19] Ashe suggests that it was pressure from this alternative group that led to the declaration of Mary as *Theotokos* at the Council of Ephesus in 431, as a way of both accommodating and controlling Marian devotion within the official Church. Although Ashe acknowledges that some of his speculations are 'historical fiction',[20] there is at least one piece of extant evidence that such women's cults did exist on the margins of the Early Church, and that they were condemned as heresies. Epiphanius, writing in the late fourth century, refers to the cult of the Collyridians, in which women priests made offerings of bread to Mary. He goes on to refute the idea that any woman, even Mary, could be a priest, and then makes a distinction between the veneration due to Mary, and the worship due to God – a distinction the Catholic Church has upheld ever since.[21]

The reference to the Collyridians invites reflection in engagement with Irigaray's argument that women's religious symbols and practices focus not on blood sacrifice but on the earth's fertility. Challenging what she sees as Girard's exclusively androcentric understanding of religion, Irigaray argues that it was only with the emergence of patriarchal religion that blood rituals took the place of grain offerings in religious rites. She writes, 'In a patriarchal regime, religion is expressed through rites of sacrifice or atonement. In women's history, religion is entangled with cultivation of the earth, of the body, of life, of peace.'[22]

Irigaray's speculative hypothesis is borne out by the anthropological research of Nancy Jay, who argues that blood sacrifice is a substitution for childbirth, in establishing patriarchal rather than matriarchal genealogies. The blood of the sacrifice takes the place of the blood of childbirth in creating social bonds between fathers and sons, which eliminates the significance of the maternal role. Jay refers to 'an affinity between blood sacrificial religion and those social systems that make the relation between father and son the basis of social order and continuity'.[23] She goes on to suggest that 'purely matrilineal ancestor cults, although equally concerned with enduring social continuity, do not depend on blood sacrifice as their "crucial" ritual, even though offerings of food are commonly important.'[24] Jay argues that the historical development of the idea of apostolic succession with the Christian

priesthood being defined in terms of an exclusively male genealogy, the increasing institutionalization of the Church, and the
emergence of a theological understanding of the Eucharist as
sacrifice, go hand in hand. Thus she suggests a close relationship
between the patriarchal succession of the priesthood and the
sacrifice of the Eucharist as a blood bond between men. If one
accepts this hypothesis, then the cult of the Collyridians points
to another, woman-centred religious world, in which a maternal
genealogy between Mary and her priestly daughters was fostered
through offerings of bread rather than blood, that is, through
celebrating the earth's fertility rather than sacrifice.

But if blood sacrifice and fertility offerings are gendered forms
of worship, then the Catholic liturgy does include symbols of
both blood and fertility which might yet become the locus of a
revitalized liturgical life in which sexual difference can be fully
celebrated as part of the goodness of God's creation. The gifts of
bread and wine are offered as fruit of the earth and fruit of the
vine. It is the fruit of the harvest that becomes spiritual food, so
that there is a symbolic association between the body of Christ
and the fertility of the earth. Not only that, but because Christ
was born from Mary alone, there has always been a sense in the
Catholic tradition that the flesh of Christ and the flesh of Mary
are one, and that Mary is therefore also bodily present in the
Eucharist.

This means that the Eucharist cannot in any straightforward
way be understood as the self-giving of the male body of Christ
which necessitates a male priest to make it symbolically coherent
– although this is one of the arguments used by the Catholic
Church against women's ordination. Christ is human flesh and
blood and Christ is also the fruit of the earth. The Eucharist
symbolizes his sacrifice on the cross, but it also symbolizes
his birth from Mary, and his identification with the nurturing
and regenerative power of nature. If the masculine religious

imagination invites us to reflect on the sacrifice of Christ, the feminine religious imagination invites us to reflect on the birth of Christ and the fecundity of the Eucharist. Together, the male priest and the female priest symbolize the holistic unity of creation and redemption, in which the whole cosmos is created and transformed through the incarnate love of God for the world.

But to acknowledge and celebrate this all-encompassing truth, the men of the Church would have to recognize what they have never been able to accept: that if all things are created and redeemed in Christ, then that includes not just the pagan mind represented by Plato and Aristotle, who have found a space of privilege in the Christian tradition, but also the pagan body represented by the maternal cults and their priestesses. God is beyond the gods and goddesses of the ancient world, but God also reveals the implicit truth in both these concepts of the divine. Women as well as men need a space of bodily self-expression in worship, a space in which all the particular symbolic associations of the female body – fertility, childbirth, female sexuality, lactation, menstruation, nurture, menopause – find forms of expression alongside the images associated with male worship. But women's religion stands in need of redemption no less than men's religion, and this is where religious feminism risks romanticizing and distorting the historical record. So what might constitute the redemption of women's religion in Christ?

Baptismal births

When we speak of perfect worlds of peace and harmony, we are always speaking in a Utopian sense. Whether we use the imagery of a perfect past associated with Eden, or of a perfect future associated with Heaven, we are in the realm of imagination where past and future worlds are dreamed into being. Without such dreams, we cannot make meaning and significance out of life. But in reality, there never has been a golden age on earth, and if feminine rituals are less prone to sacrificial violence than masculine ones, women are not immune to the frenzy and violence that form the dark underside of spirituality. One only has to read Euripides' *The Bacchae* to get a sense of the bloodlust that can hold women in its grip at the peak of spiritual self-abandonment. Some would argue that women are the victims rather than the perpetrators of these rituals, but to absolve femininity of any implication in violence or sin is to render the woman entirely passive in whatever mythical or fictional stories we use to explain the existence of evil in the world. In the interpretation of the Genesis myth, to make Eve the victim of collusive power exercised between the phallic serpent, the patriarchal God of Israel and the masculinity of Adam is to go from the one extreme, which attributes all responsibility for the Fall to Eve, to another extreme, which attributes no responsibility at all to her, so that she is the victim rather than the agent of her own story.

Genesis invites us to recognize the agency and responsibility of both sexes, so that however we explain our original orientation to rebellion and wrong, as men and women we are equally implicated – vulnerable to temptation and open to grace, full participants in the story of the Fall and redemption. But if this is true it must find liturgical expression, and in Catholicism, where blood symbolism is an important part of worship and liturgy, the influence of gender becomes particularly significant.

The relationship between the female body and blood is more complex than that between the male body and blood, given that the male body only bleeds when wounded, whereas the female body bleeds regularly as a sign of fertility. A woman's bleeding body is a complex language of signs which she must learn to interpret. It can mean disease but it can also mean good health. It communicates to her that she has reached sexual maturity with the onset of menstruation, and that she is entering a new phase of life with the menopause, when she no longer bleeds. If she longs for pregnancy, then the sight of blood means disappointment and loss, but if she is afraid of pregnancy then her monthly period is a sign of reassurance and relief. All this means that in rites that retain some form of blood symbolism – as the Mass does – there will be potent although perhaps unconscious messages encoded in the language and rituals we perform. When the priest says, 'This is my body, this is my blood', his male body perhaps inevitably suggests the wounding and death of Christ on the cross, for how else can a man offer his blood except by offering his woundedness? But if a woman says, 'This is my body, this is my blood', her female body is more likely to suggest fertility and childbirth than sacrifice and death. Is this uncomfortable for men because inevitably it also implies sexuality? Girard argues that men's fear of blood leads them to associate the bleeding, sexual female body with violence.[25] Aquinas argues that one reason against women priests is 'lest men's sexual desires be aroused'.[26]

But even without such male projections, for women themselves childbirth is closely associated with suffering and death. This is why, if Eve is to stand beside Adam and celebrate her bodiliness, if she is to say as an affirmation of faith that 'I believe in the resurrection of the body and the life of the world to come', she needs symbols that promise resurrection, wholeness and liberation from the suffering of birth and motherhood. That is why she needs to look at Mary, her younger sister and daughter in Christ, not through the eyes of celibate men but through the eyes of her own womanly self. And what might she see?

In one of the niches in the Pantheon, there is an imposing statue of a mother and her daughter. The mother is a vast figure, protective but also severe. Her daughter is moulded around the contours of classical Greek and Roman sculpture, so that she might be a robed goddess. The statue is of St Anne and her daughter, the Virgin Mary, by the eighteenth-century sculptor Lorenzo Toni. It serves as a potent reminder that Mary has not always been 'alone of all her sex', although it is unusual to find such a recent example of this iconography. In the Middle Ages, Anne was the most popular saint after Mary, and together they stood at the centre of a vast extended family of women saints. The medieval historian David Herlihy writes of the feminization of sainthood in the Middle Ages.[27] When the men of the Church were riding into battle and beginning the transition to a mercantile economy, the women who stayed behind were forming the Church in their own image, elevating those saints who could express something of their changing roles and social status. How does Anne fit into the story of Mary, and how might this mother–daughter pair offer an alternative religious vision that gives symbolic expression to the realities of women's lives?

To discover this other Mary, we need to journey from the Pantheon to Trastevere, the medieval part of the city, where fashionable restaurants, car mechanics' workshops and hardware shops jostle for space amidst the cobbled lanes, and Romans and tourists mingle in the balmy afternoon. Here we find the Church of Santa Maria in Trastevere, where a series of wall mosaics depicts Mary's story.

Notes

1. Stephen Benko, *The Virgin Goddess: Studies in the Pagan and Christian Roots of Mariology* (New York: E. J. Brill, 1993), p. 4.
2. Quoted in Thomas Livius, *The Blessed Virgin in the Fathers of the First Six Centuries* (London: Burns & Oates; New York: Benziger Brothers, 1893), p. 56.
3. See Robin Lane Fox, *Pagans and Christians in the Mediterranean World from the Second Century AD to the Conversion of Constantine* (London: Viking Press, 1986), pp. 347–8.
4. See Augustine of Hippo, *Concerning the City of God against the Pagans*,

ed. David Knowles, trans. Henry Bettenson (London: Penguin, 1981), Book II.4, pp. 51–2.

5. See Firmicus Maternicus, *The Error of the Pagan Religions*, trans. and annotated by Clarence A. Forbes (New York and Ramsey, NJ: Newman Press, 1970).

6. See Fox, *Pagans and Christians*, pp. 372–4.

7. Jürgen Moltmann, 'The Inviting Unity of the Triune God', in Claude Geffré and Jean Pièrre Jossua (eds), *Monotheism, Concilium 177* (Edinburgh: T. & T. Clark, 1985): pp. 50–8, p. 55.

8. Geoffrey Ashe, *The Virgin* (London: Routledge & Kegan Paul, 1976), p. 145.

9. Lynn White, Jr, 'The Historical Roots of our Ecological Crisis', in Mary Heather MacKinnon and Moni McIntyre (eds), *Readings in Ecology and Feminist Theology* (Kansas City, KS: Sheed & Ward, 1995): pp. 25–35.

10. See René Girard, *Violence and the Sacred*, trans. Patrick Gregory (Baltimore, MD: The Johns Hopkins University Press, 1977), pp. 34–5.

11. See Julia Kristeva, *Tales of Love*, and *Powers of Horror – An Essay on Abjection*, trans. Leon S. Roudiez (New York: Columbia University Press, 1982).

12. See Kristeva, *Powers of Horror*, pp. 90–112.

13. John A. Phillips, *Eve: The History of an Idea* (San Francisco, CA: Harper & Row, 1984), p. 15, quoted in Anne Baring and Jules Cashford, *The Myth of the Goddess: Evolution of an Image* (London: Arkana, Penguin, 1993), p. 495.

14. Kristeva, *Powers of Horror*, pp. 113–32.

15. Kristeva, *Tales of Love*, p. 263.

16. See Irigaray, *Thinking the Difference*.

17. See Nicholas Perry and Loreto Echeverría, *Under the Heel of Mary* (London: Routledge, 1988).

18. See Warner, *Alone of All her Sex*.

19. Ashe, *The Virgin*, p. 195.

20. Ibid., p. 161.

21. See Hilda Graef, *Mary: A History of Doctrine and Devotion*, comb. edn (London: Sheed & Ward, 1994), p. 73.

22. Irigaray, *Thinking the Difference*, p. 11.

23. Nancy Jay, 'Sacrifice as Remedy for Having Been Born of Woman', in Clarissa W. Atkinson, Constance H. Buchanan and Margaret R.

Miles (eds), *Immaculate and Powerful: The Female in Sacred Image and Social Reality* (Boston, MA: Crucible, 1987): pp. 283–309, p. 285.

24. Ibid., p. 291.
25. See Girard, *Violence and the Sacred*, pp. 34–5.
26. See Thomas Aquinas, *Summa Theologiae: A Concise Translation*, ed. Timothy McDermott (London: Methuen, 1992), p. 450.
27. See David Herlihy, 'The Family and Religious Ideology in Medieval Europe', in D. Herlily and A. Molho (eds), *Women, Family and Society in Medieval Europe* (New York and Oxford: Berghahn Books, 1995): pp. 154–73.

Mosaic of the Virgin Enthroned, façade of Church of Santa Maria in Trastevere

4

The Maternal Church:
Santa Maria in Trastevere

The birth of Mary

The twelfth-century basilica of Santa Maria in Trastevere stands on the site of an earlier, fourth-century, church, making it the oldest place of Christian worship in Rome. There is a legend that in 38 BC, when a hospice for wounded Roman soldiers – the *Taberna Meritoria* – stood on the same site, oil gushed from the ground and flowed into the River Tiber. This event, known as *fons olei* ('fountain of oil') is chronicled in some ancient texts, and early Christians interpreted it as foretelling the birth of Christ. The mosaic of the nativity in the apse of the basilica shows the *Taberna Meritoria* and the oil flowing into the Tiber.

Set in a bustling square beside one of the oldest fountains in Rome, only the basilica's seventeenth-century arched porch sets it apart from its medieval surroundings. It lacks the gaudy assertiveness of some of Rome's other churches, but it is perhaps one of the city's finest jewels: a treasure trove of maternal feminine imagery, which invites reflection on the forgotten presence of women in the story of the incarnation.

As one approaches, the church's twelfth-century façade hints at what is to come. It is adorned with a mosaic that shows Mary enthroned, breast-feeding the infant Christ, while ten women come towards her bearing offerings. I think the women represent the wise and foolish bridesmaids in the parable in Matthew 25, but if so there is no hint of judgement and condemnation. In Matthew's Gospel, Christ says that the five bridesmaids whose lamps have gone out are refused entry to the wedding feast, but in this mosaic all ten figures wear haloes and approach Christ and his mother in reverence and tenderness.

The mosaics inside the church are by the artist Pietro Cavallini, contemporary of Giotto, and their exquisite craftsmanship reflects the changes in style and perspective that mark out the thirteenth century as a time of transformation in Western art. Newly restored, they shimmer with the gold of the sun and exude the timeless quality of the incarnation. The vault shows the Virgin in Majesty with Christ, above a frieze of sheep representing Christ and the apostles. The apse is decorated with five scenes from the Life of the Virgin – her Nativity, the Annunciation, the Nativity of Christ, the Presentation of Christ in the Temple, and the Dormition of the Virgin. (See p. 115).

The latter is a frequent theme in icons: it shows Mary at the moment of her death or 'falling asleep', surrounded by the apostles, with Christ standing beside her and cradling her infant soul in his arms. It is an image that mirrors scenes of Mary with the infant Christ, so that it brings to completion a sense of the incarnation as an encompassing expression of maternal love: Anne's love for her daughter, Mary's love for her son and Christ's maternal love for his mother's soul. A poem by the Victorian poet John Bannister Tabb evokes this sense of Christ welcoming his mother into heaven:

> Behold! the Mother bird
> The Fledgling's voice hath heard!
>   He calls anew,
>   'It was thy breast

> That warmed the nest
> From whence I flew.
> Upon a loftier tree
> Of life I wait for thee;
> Rise, Mother-dove, and come,
> Thy Fledgeling calls thee home!'

The modern Church has lost sight of the birthing images that come before and after the incarnation itself – the birth of Mary to Anne, and the 'birth' of Mary's soul into the arms of Christ.

Images of Mary's birth are a rich resource for re-visioning the Christian story in a way that is expressive of women's experience but still faithful to the Catholic tradition. The mosaic of the Nativity of the Virgin in Santa Maria in Trastevere shows St Anne reclining upon a birthing bed, robed in the royal colours of blue and red. She inclines her head towards her two women attendants who gaze back at her as they bring food to a table – a basket of bread and a jug, perhaps anticipating the bread and wine of the body of Christ. Sitting at Anne's feet, another woman holds the infant Mary while a fourth pours water into a bath. Again, perhaps the image is suggestive of baptism. Mary turns her head towards her mother, so that the meeting of eyes links together mother, baby and friends in bonds of love.

It is a scene suffused with serenity and tenderness, showing the way of Christ being prepared not by rugged prophets and heroic men but by women in that most bodily and womanly of worlds – the birthing chamber. Already the peace of Christ broods protectively over the scene, as Mary's birth signals the dawn of the incarnation. Here is a birth without violence and bloodshed, without sweat and labour, without the tearing apart of the mother's flesh and the limp exhaustion that comes afterwards. Some might argue that this makes the scene unreal and impossibly remote from women's actual experiences of childbirth, but for all its quiet grandeur the picture is inclusive, drawing every woman into its peaceful solidarity. The picture speaks to me, as a woman who has experienced the mess and struggle of giving birth, not of denial but of promise. God is with us in our mothering, and we are not abandoned in the suffering we share with Eve. The newborn arrives among us as a sign of hope amidst a tide of pain and blood, but one day there will be hope without pain and life will be given without the shedding of blood.

For women who have access to reliable contraception and good health-care facilities, childbirth has been liberated from its terrors. But for the poor women of two-thirds of the world, fertility and childbearing are still associated with poverty, pain and death. Every minute, one woman dies from causes related to pregnancy and childbirth. Two-thirds of the world's pregnant women are anaemic. For less than the world spends in one week on arms, every woman in the world could be given access to basic health-care in pregnancy and childbirth.

In the thirteenth century, when the mosaics in Santa Maria in Trastevere were created, Western women still confronted their own mortality and capacity for suffering most acutely in child-birth and motherhood. The cluster of maternal images surrounding the story of Christ offered a different way of seeing the world, a vision that gave concrete hope to Eve's suffering. Mary, the New Eve, was the fulfilment of God's promise to Eve, and if that promise was yet to be brought to completion and perfection, it had already been made tangibly, visibly manifest in the incarnation.

The story of St Anne

The English writer, poet and campaigner for women's rights Alice Meynell was a frequent visitor to Italy and a convert to

Catholicism. Describing the Birth of the Virgin in art, she wrote in 1923:

> When English readers, or English people in galleries abroad, leave what is for them the safe old ground of the four Evangelists, all the rest is indifferent to them; they are either a little curious or a little incurious – generally a little incurious.... It is more than probable that many a 'Nativity of the Virgin' is taken for a variant of the Nativity of Christ, painted by some master who had become weary of the presence of the ox and the ass, had had enough of the loft or the cave, of the shepherds and Saint Joseph, and was minded to provide the birth of the Saviour with credible witnesses in the form of women busy in sick-room offices about the Mother and Child. And yet those women are, in Tradition, all provided with names – friends and handmaids of St Anne.... Nothing remains, in the popular mind of our country, except the long habit of the name of Anne: Mary and Anne, names of the fairer daughter and the fair mother, and Mary Anne, the name whereby a child was placed under the double patronage. But few of the Annes of modern England have referred their grave and homely monosyllable to the wife of Joachim and the aged mother of Mary.[1]

Meynell's words anticipate a growing interest among some feminist scholars in the story of Mary and her apocryphal mother, St Anne or Anna, who for centuries has been all but forgotten in the Western Church. There is no reference to Anne in the New Testament, but she first occurs in a second-century text, the *Protevangelium of James*, which includes an account of the life of Mary. Although this was widely circulated in the Early Church, it was condemned by Jerome in the fourth century and remained relatively obscure in the West until the Middle Ages, although the cult of St Anne has been continuous in the Eastern Church. Its revival in the West might be due to the influence of Eastern Christians fleeing the Muslim conquests. The earliest known image of St Anne in the West is in the Church of Santa Maria Antiqua in Rome, and it dates back to about 650. By the late Middle Ages devotion to St Anne was widespread in the Western Church so that she was second in popularity only to her daughter, and the *Protevangelium* inspired a proliferation of legends and artistic representations of the life of the Virgin. The five mosaics in Santa Maria in Trastevere feature only some of the scenes commonly found in these narrative compositions – others such as those in the basilica of Santa Maria Maggiore include many more events relating to the life of Mary and her parents, Anne and Joachim. As an interesting aside it is worth noting that in Santa Maria Maggiore, the eighteenth-century fresco of the Birth of the Virgin includes two men, with Joachim in the foreground. (In Chapter 5 I will explore how the male figure came to define and eventually eclipse the female figures in the Christian story.)

The *Protevangelium* describes how Joachim, a wealthy elder of Israel, has his offering rejected by the temple priest because he has no children. The humiliated Joachim retreats into the wilderness, and at home his elderly wife Anna laments the double grief of her widowhood and her sterility. But Anna's handmaid, Judith, persuades her to set aside her mourning garments and to dress in bridal clothes for the day of the Lord, and thus attired, Anna goes into the garden. Sitting under a laurel tree in which sparrows are nesting, she bemoans her barrenness and prays for a child. In a scene reminiscent of Luke's account of the Annunciation, an angel appears and tells her that she will conceive, and that she must go and meet her husband who has been told by an angel to come back to the city. The couple meet and embrace at the city gates, and Anna becomes pregnant. She gives birth to a daughter,

Mary, and when the child is three years old her parents take her to the temple, where she lives until puberty, at which age she must leave, lest she defile the temple. The high priest calls together widowers in the region to find a husband for Mary. A dove emerges from the staff of Joseph and alights on his head, which the high priest takes as a sign that this is the man chosen by God to marry the Virgin. Joseph reluctantly agrees to marry the young girl although he is afraid that this will make him a laughing stock. When he returns from a journey and finds Mary pregnant, he is shocked and ashamed. Putting on sackcloth, he cries out,

> Has the story of Adam been re-enacted in me? For in the very moment Adam was glorifying God, the serpent came and found Eve alone and deceived her; the same thing has happened to me.' And Joseph put aside his sackcloth, called Mary and said to her, 'You who were cared for by God, why have you done this? How could you forget your God? Why have you so humiliated yourself? You who were brought up in the Holy of Holies and received food from the hand of an angel?[22]

Mary weeps and pleads her innocence, and an angel appears to reassure Joseph. The *Protevangelium* then follows the birth narratives of the gospels, but includes the story of Salome, the midwife who refuses to believe that a Virgin has given birth and insists on examining Mary, upon which her hand is burned. An angel instructs her to touch the child, and she is healed.

There are clear echoes in the *Protevangelium* of the story of Hannah and Samuel in the Old Testament. Its theological purpose is to situate Mary in the context of earlier biblical figures, in order to show the incarnation as the consummation of God's promise through history. But the text was popular because it filled in the gaps in the biblical story, providing the resources for a rich tradition of devotions, art and folklore, which has coexisted, at some times more comfortably than at others, alongside the official doctrines and biblical teachings of the Church. In the imaginative climate of medieval devotion, the *Protevangelium* flourished into a rich collection of legends and folklore, in which most of the main protagonists in the incarnation apart from Christ himself were women. The *Protevangelium* depicts Joseph in a somewhat dubious light, as one who is ambivalent about his role and embarrassed by his young wife's condition. In medieval mystery plays he is sometimes portrayed as a comic figure, quick to accuse Mary and bemused by the position in which he finds himself. Herlihy points to the absence of Joseph from the writings of the Early Church, and the lack of male role-models in medieval ideas of sainthood. He writes that 'after the thirteenth century ... there are virtually no prominent male saints, and none who might serve as an example to married men and heads of households. Patriarchy did not rule the ranks of the blessed, at least not in the late Middle Ages.'[3]

It is in the context of this maternal era in Christian history that modern women might situate our reflections on Mary and Anne and their potential relevance for women today. In a patriarchal world in which sons have always been more welcome than daughters, the birth of the Virgin breaks the patterns of history. According to the *Protevangelium*, Anne 'said to the midwife, "What have I given birth to?" And she said, "It is a girl." And Anna said, "My soul has been exalted this day." '[4] Anne's exultant welcome to her baby daughter is perhaps unique in the records and stories of patriarchal religion, for who in a family of male divinities, fathers and sons welcomes the birth of a daughter?

Maternal conceptions

The popularity of St Anne in the Middle Ages was related to theological concerns about the doctrine of the Immaculate Conception – the belief that Mary was conceived without original sin. This became a topic of heated theological debate from the twelfth century, although it was finally promulgated as dogma only in 1854. However, whatever the scepticism of the learned, the feast of the Immaculate Conception was celebrated from the eleventh century in England, reflecting the importance of the Virgin Mary in medieval English Catholicism. As with many of the Church's teachings on Mary, dogma has been driven by populism, with theologians being challenged to find intellectual justification for popular devotions. As we shall see, sometimes, as in the case of the Immaculate Conception, this has resulted in the dogmatic affirmation of popular beliefs. In other instances, for example with regard to the cult of St Anne, the custodians of doctrine have obliterated the cherished beliefs of the people.

St Anne was central to the iconography of the Immaculate Conception between the thirteenth and fifteenth centuries. The Embrace at the Golden Gate was symbolically identified as the moment of Mary's spiritual conception, and it became a popular way of depicting the Immaculate Conception in art. One of the loveliest and earliest images of this type is that by Giotto in the Arena Chapel in Padua. Some believed that Mary, like Christ, was a virginal conception, but the prevailing view was that Joachim and Anne went home and had intercourse, and that was when Mary was bodily conceived by her mother. The idea that the venerable parents of the Virgin Mary would stoop so low as to have sex in old age was shocking to a Christian culture imbued with the belief that even marital sex had the taint of sin about it, so it was widely believed that Anne and Joachim were acting out of obedience to God, and that they found the physical act a necessary but distasteful duty. Nevertheless, it remains true that whenever St Anne appears in Christian art and devotion, she symbolizes a sexually active, married woman whose status was at one time second only to that of her virgin daughter. Today, the image of the Embrace at the Golden Gate is a voluptuous, tender celebration of married love, which is ripe for reclamation by those who seek more positive representations of marriage and sexuality within the Christian tradition.

But there are other, even more potent images associated with the Immaculate Conception, and these are known as *Anna Selbdritt* or *St Anne Trinitarian.* In these images, St Anne, Mary and the infant Christ are represented as an earthly trinity, symbolizing the incarnational dimension of the heavenly Trinity.[5] If the divine soul of Christ was associated with the patriarchal family grouping of father, son and spirit, his human body was associated with the matriarchal grouping of mother, daughter and son. Although on the face of it this upholds the hierarchical, gendered relationship between masculine divinity and feminine humanity, Caroline Walker Bynum suggests that it also provided a sense of identification and affinity between the female flesh and the humanity of Christ.[6] Modern interpreters sometimes point to the Holy Family of Mary, Joseph and Christ as an earthly trinity, but such a suggestion reinforces rather than subverts the patriarchal tradition. Joseph becomes a father figure whose presence mirrors the patriarchy of God and erases the imposing maternal presence of Anne who, in some medieval art, stands guard over the Virgin and her child. One of the most striking of these images is the fifteenth-century painting of the *Virgin and Child with St Anne* by Masaccio and/or Masolino in the Uffizi Gallery in Florence. The Leonardo cartoon in the National Gallery in London is a more tender depiction of the same subject.

A third set of images associated with St Anne concerns the Holy Kinship tradition, which represents a highly imaginative and convoluted attempt to account for the brothers and sisters of Christ mentioned in the gospels. How could Christ have had siblings if his mother remained a virgin? The answer was to see them as cousins rather than as immediate family, and to construct an elaborate kinship group to account for these and various other figures who are named in the gospels. Thus, it was claimed that Joachim had died and Anne had married twice more, giving birth to two more daughters named Mary. Mary Cleophas, wife of Alphaeus and mother of the Apostles James the Lesser, Simon and Judas, and Joseph the Just, was the daughter of a marriage between Anne and Cleophas. After the death of Cleophas, Anne married Salome and gave birth to Mary Salome, wife of Zebedee and mother of the apostles John and James the Greater. Not content with this extended family grouping, medieval interpreters went even further and gave names and stories to the parents of Anne – Emerentia and Stollanus. Respected theologians such as John of Eck and Jean Gerson wrote and preached on these genealogies, which inspired a genre of paintings in which Christ and his young companions are depicted in the midst of large groups of women – grandmothers, mothers, sisters and daughters clustered around the matriarchal figure of St Anne.[7]

Such images were never, however, without controversy, for while they might prove satisfactory in accounting for Christ's family relations, the idea of the three marriages or *trinubium* of Anne caused some consternation. Women were encouraged to remain chaste if their husbands died, and the suggestion that Anne remarried twice more after the death of Joachim suggested an incontinent desire for continued sex entirely inappropriate for the grandmother of Christ. One medieval account tells how Colette of Corbie refused to pray to St Anne because she was shocked by her three marriages. But Anne appeared to her in an apparition, surrounded by 'all her glorious progeny', and told Colette that 'although she had several times copulated in marriage no one in the whole church militant and triumphant was so adorned for his progeny and honored with fame'.[8] Thereafter, Colette had a lively devotion to Anne and her various offspring. Controversy raged around the issue until the Council of Trent forbade reference to the *trinubium*, and by the end of the sixteenth century St Anne had all but disappeared from Christian art, swept away on the related tides of the Reformation and the Counter-Reformation.

Christian matricide

In Chapter 3 I described how Kristeva traces back the origins of the Western psyche to the early process by which the people of Israel began to separate themselves from the maternal cults. In common with many cultural theorists, Kristeva draws on Freud's theory of the Oedipus complex to construct a hypothesis about the development of Western culture with its patriarchal values and androcentric norms.

In later life, Freud himself interpreted the Oedipus theory as an account of the evolution of culture.[9] He argued that humankind was undergoing a process of development from an early stage of matriarchal religions and goddess worship, through the worship of the male gods of polytheism, to the monotheism of Judaism and Protestant Christianity, and finally to a state of civilization in which religion would become redundant and science and reason alone would provide the moral and intellectual resources for the making of culture. Interestingly, he saw Catholicism as regressive in this respect, because in the Virgin and the female saints it seemed to hark back to the goddess figures of the matriarchal era.

As part of this collective oedipal process, Freud suggested that religious sacrifice had its origins in the murder of an all-powerful father by a primal horde of brothers.[10] The brothers murdered the father out of jealousy for his women, consuming his body partly in order to acquire his power, and partly through guilt over his death. This, argued Freud, constituted the psychological origins of the Eucharist.

From a modern perspective, Freud's hypotheses about religion and culture fall somewhat short of scientific criteria. Despite his resistance to religion and his commitment to science, his theories about culture have much more in common with religious myths than with scientific theories, in so far as they are psychologically compelling but lacking in any of the empirical or historical evidence that would lend them scientific credibility. Nevertheless, his influence on modern society has been far-reaching, and he has had a profound effect on Western ideas about culture, religion and sexuality. Many critical theorists find psychoanalysis a useful resource for analysing and interpreting culture, and in the case of feminist theory, critical readings of Freud are used to explore the origins and development of patriarchy. As with Freud's own theories, these are hypothetical and speculative accounts, concerned less with the reinterpretation of history than with the re-imaging of symbols.

Thus Irigaray argues that Western society is founded on a more ancient murder than that of the Freudian primal father: it is founded on an original act of matricide, which involves the symbolic murder of the mother as the precondition for a patriarchal civilization founded exclusively on masculine and paternal values. Analyzing the readings of Western philosophy and psychoanalysis from Plato through Freud to Jacques Derrida and Jacques Lacan, Irigaray sees a persistent denial of the material origins of life in the maternal womb and a failure to acknowledge the dependence of culture on the materiality of the body and the earth. Platonic ideals of goodness, truth and beauty are, she argues, the projections of a masculine culture, which seeks to transcend the maternal body associated with women and the earth, in order to model itself on a set of abstract and rationalized values associated with the father and God.

But Irigaray repeats Freud's mistake, by offering a decontextualized and ahistorical account of culture, which oversimplifies the picture. It may indeed be true that Greek philosophy and its modern and postmodern derivatives are highly dualistic and androcentric – and Christianity has played no small part in perpetuating these values. But alongside its Platonic philosophies, Catholic Christianity also understood the incarnation largely in terms of maternal symbolism – Christ was born of a human mother, and his bodily presence is perpetuated in the eucharistic offerings of the maternal Church. When we look at medieval Christianity, we are looking through a doorway into a world in which the symbolic presence of the maternal body was potent and pervasive. If the role of the mother was, as Irigaray argues, negated and destroyed in the making of Western culture from the time of Plato, it was to a very large extent rehabilitated in the sacraments and symbols of the premodern Church. But since the Second Vatican Council the idea of the pilgrim people of God has to some extent replaced that of Holy Mother Church, so that modern religious culture lacks any sense of a divinized maternal power. From the perspectives of both secularism and Christianity, those powerful mothers of the medieval church are distant and even alien figures. If, as many feminist theorists and theologians argue, there is a relationship between our symbolic relationship to the maternal body, our attitudes to nature and the environment, and the social and sexual representation of women, then it is worth asking how these aspects of medieval culture disintegrated in the making of the modern world.

From sacramentality to morality

Up until the late Middle Ages, Christianity was a religion not of morality but of cosmic transformation. Of course, it had moral rules and often severe penalties for violating these, but Christ was primarily experienced not through the morally upright life of the respectable citizen, but through the grace of God, which suffused creation with beauty and meaning. The sacraments caught up this material world and made it the particular locus of the encounter between the human and the divine, between the language and rituals of human worship and the materialization of the divine presence. The nurturing body that mediated this divine presence was that of the maternal Church.

Nature participated in this sanctification of the mother, for the earth herself was maternal and, like the body of Mary, was restored to virginal purity in Christ. Medieval liturgies for the Feast of St Anne, celebrated on 26 July, are rich in images of nature. Anne is like the fertile soil, which blossoms in anticipation of the incarnation, spreading to the ends of the earth the fragrance of the incarnate Word. Premodern Christians inhabited a numinous world in which holy wells, sacred sites and places of pilgrimage communicated a sense of a physical universe that had been permeated with the power and presence of God through the incarnation. In addition, the liturgical year formed a spiralling dance of time, which followed the linear movement of history while revolving around the cycles of nature. Thus the Christian year is still an intricate weaving together of different forms of time, in which Christmas follows the regular pattern of calendrical time measured by the sun, while Easter is measured in lunar time. These different forms of time are sometimes interpreted as masculine and feminine, so that historical or calendrical time represents a linear, masculine order, while lunar time symbolizes the fertile cycles of nature and the female body. They might also be associated with the contrast between biblical mythology with its linear story of history in which time has a beginning and an end, and other religious myths which see the universe more in terms of eternal cycles of birth, death and regeneration.

So one might argue that the sacraments and seasons of Catholicism represent a synthesis between the Hebrew and pagan worlds, between the historical religious consciousness of the people of Israel, and the cyclical cosmology of pagan religion. Through this encounter, a new religion comes into being. The ethical monotheism of the Hebrews is reconciled with the maternal cults of the ancient world, creating the potential for a new way of living in which the maternal body of the Church gives birth to a transformed ethical and religious community reconciling Greek and Jew, male and female, slave and free, in a harmony of being that resonates with the original harmony and diversity of creation. If this reconciliation was never accomplished, it is nevertheless true that Christianity baptized the pagan maternal flesh in many ways, so that the final destruction of paganism by Christianity happened not with the conversion of Constantine but with the Reformation.

In its rejection of the sacramentality of the medieval Church, Protestantism purged Christianity of its material and its maternal dimensions. It thus severed the connection between creation and incarnation, initiating a form of Christianity whose worship was based not on the sacramentality of a created order suffused with the incarnational presence of God but on the moral authority of an abstract and transcendent Word. God became identified with a remote and authoritarian father figure ruling over an increasingly rationalized and masculine world, and it did not take long for the men of the Western world to recognize that, ultimately, such a God is simply an adjunct to the power of reason and serves little useful purpose in a functional and demystified universe. With the philosophy of Kant and the Enlightenment, the

Western world-view became one in which the man of reason came to occupy the place previously occupied by God.

More than three centuries after the Reformation, when Freud peered into the Western unconscious, he found a turmoil of frustrated desire and violence associated with the forbidden relationship to the mother. The psychologist D. W. Winnicott suggests that the maternal relationship constitutes a transitional dimension of the psyche, a space of play associated with creativity, religion and imagination.[11] In a secularized and technological culture we have forgotten the grace inherent in playful creative imaginings, which have neither purpose nor productivity beyond their own epiphanies of insight and joy. The maternal memory still haunts us in the music, art and architecture of Catholic Europe, but these have become symbols devoid of content, not spaces of play but objects situated at a great historical and psychological distance from the modern mind.

Reforming symbols

While the Reformation abolished the sacramental body in an overt and often violent way, the Counter-Reformation was a more subtle and insidious way of achieving a similar end. The Council of Trent set about responding to some of the criticisms of the reformers by putting its own house in order. In a Decree of 1563 it abolished all practices, images and observances that were deemed to be occasions of 'dangerous error to the uneducated'. It banished 'every superstition' and 'all lasciviousness' from the cult of the saints. And it warned that 'the unlettered people' must be taught that divinity could not be represented or seen 'by the eyes of the body, or be portrayed by colours and figures'.[12] The declaration stipulated that 'figures shall not be painted or adorned with a beauty exciting to lust'. Sacred images should involve 'nothing that is profane, nothing indecorous'.[13] One consequence of this new prudery was the modification of Michelangelo's fresco of the Last Judgement in the Sistine Chapel. Discreet drapery was added to the naked bodies by the painter Daniele da Volterra, who was thereafter known as 'il Braghettone' (the breeches-maker).

Here we have the creeping reinforcement of the barrier between the sacred and the profane, between the polluting and the pure, which Kristeva suggests is associated with the rejection of the maternal cults and the affirmation of the patriarchal law. St Anne, thrice married, rushing to fall into her husband's arms at the Golden Gate and conceiving the Mother of Christ in the sexual expression of married love, takes on the aura of Eve – profane, lascivious, exciting to lust. The Council of Trent forbade images such as the Embrace at the Golden Gate, since they were believed to detract from the spiritual significance of the Immaculate Conception.

Searching for a new form of iconography, the artists of the sixteenth and seventeenth centuries gave rise to a tradition that has persisted ever since in representations of the Virgin. No longer could the Immaculate Conception be pictured in ways that celebrated the redemption and the sanctification of the material world and of women's bodies in Mary, her mother and her son. Drawing on biblical images and perhaps subliminally influenced by changing cultural perceptions of women, artists such as Velázquez began to depict the Immaculate Conception as an idealized young woman, lacking even the child in her arms, floating upwards to God, crowned in stars and standing on a crescent moon. Writing about such images, Christo Kolvachi says that

> The new iconographic type, with the Virgin and God the Father as the main protagonists, first gained currency in the sixteenth century in the shape of a complex, many-figured symbolic composition. The Virgin is generally shown in the

skies, standing or kneeling before God the Father, and surrounded by doctors of theology who debate on the nature of
the doctrine, supporting their arguments with their writings.[14]

Now, at last, Mary had truly become alone of all her sex, not a
woman or a mother but a transcendent ideal, the eternal feminine
whose image is produced not by the material realities of women's
lives but by the projections and disputes of doctors of theology.
One senses this shift in the artistic imagination if one compares
the mosaics in Santa Maria in Trastevere with a later seventeenth-
century painting of the Assumption by Domenichino, set into
the church's wooden ceiling. This shows Mary sitting on clouds
and surrounded by cherubs, raising her arms and lifting her
eyes to heaven. It is an image which sets transcendence against
immanence, heaven against earth, and spirit against body.

The transition from the maternal community of the Middle
Ages to the solitary perfection of the Immaculate Conception
reflects the changing image of woman in a culture that had started
to be defined exclusively in masculine terms. Consider, for
example, the writings of another art critic, the Italian Adolfo
Venturi, writing at the beginning of the twentieth century.
Venturi compares images of the Nativity of the Virgin with
ancient Roman and Greek bas-relief, which depict the horoscope
of a child in the presence of the Fates. But he says that by the
sixteenth century such images were neglected in favour of more
imposing artistic themes. He writes:

That age tended to enlarge and to give dignity – the dignity
of the world – to its scenes of art; it sought magnificent
composition, and an equality of nobility amongst the figures.
Doubtless such a temper was ill-suited to the scene of the
Nativity of Mary. The incident was simple, a household event,
a matter of women, lacking the heroic, and wanting especially

the weight of noble character. What we moderns call a genre subject was precisely that of the birth-chamber in the house of Joachim and Anne; and the sixteenth century sacrificed 'genre' to its own magnificence.[15]

In a society increasingly concerned to represent itself in terms of the values of heroism, magnificence, nobility and 'the dignity of the world', women's lives were devalued, robbed of their social and religious significance, and ultimately 'sacrificed' to the heroic aspirations of masculinity.

In a side chapel of Santa Maria in Trastevere, there is a sixteenth-century painting of the Counter-Reformation by P. Cati, which suggests some of the contradictions and tensions inherent in the transition from the maternal Church of the medieval era to the more rationalized and masculine Church of the Counter-Reformation. In the background, this painting shows ranks of men dressed in black, seated in front of the cardinals, with the Holy Spirit descending in one corner in the form of a dove. In the foreground is what I can only take to be a rather bizarre symbolization of the Church, represented by a motley collection of women. One woman sits to the right of the picture in a papal crown, wielding a sword with the body of a man at her feet. Another woman in a helmet cradles an axe while beside her a mother holds twins in her arms. Behind the female papal figure, a woman holds a gold chalice. Just to the left and in the front of the picture, there is a globe of the world and a pile of books. I have tried in vain to find information about this painting, but it invites the imagination to run riot. Does it represent the triumphal fecundity and power of Holy Mother Church, or does it rather represent ranks of clerics ready to impose order on the pagan dissolution and feminine chaos of the laity? Either way, it is a strange juxtaposition of images, which communicates much about the changes in perspective of the Counter-Reformation.

To explore the nature of these changes, and to consider ways in which they affected the representation of both women and nature in the making of the modern world, we need to look more closely at the art and ideas of the seventeenth century. So for the next stage of this pilgrimage we visit the basilica of Santa Maria Maggiore and the Villa Borghese, looking at the Counter-Reformation through the eyes of women to see beyond the blind-spots of the men who reformed the Church in their image.

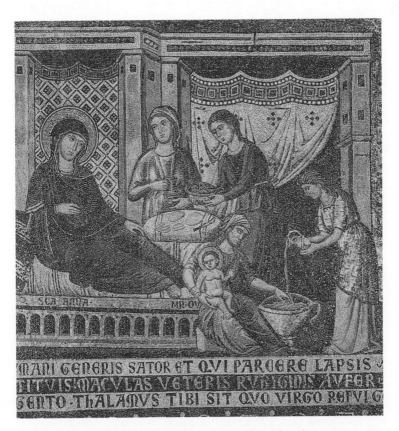

Birth of the Virgin, Pietro Cavallini, Church
of Santa Maria in Trastevere

Notes

1. Alice Meynell, *Mary, the Mother of Jesus* (London: Medici Society, 1923), pp. 30–1.
2. 'The Protevangelium of James', in Buby, *Mary of Galilee*, pp. 44–5.
3. Herlihy, 'The Family and Religious Ideology', p. 171.
4. 'Protevangelium', in Buby, *Mary of Galilee*, p. 40.
5. See Pamela Sheingorn, 'Appropriating the Holy Kinship: Gender and Family History', in Kathleen Ashley and Pamela Sheingorn (eds), *Interpreting Cultural Symbols: Saint Anne in Late Medieval Society* (Athens and London: University of Georgia Press, 1997): pp. 169–98.
6. See Caroline Walker Bynum, '"... and Woman His Humanity": Female Imagery in the Religious Writing of the Late Middle Ages', in *Fragmentation and Redemption: Essays on Gender and the Human Body in Medieval Religion* (New York: Zone Books, 1994): pp. 151–79.
7. See Tom Brandenbarg, 'St Anne and her Family', in Lène Dresen-Coenders (ed.), *Saints and She-Devils: Images of Women in the 15th and 16th Centuries* (London: Rubicon Press, 1987): pp. 101–27.
8. Kathleen Ashley, 'Image and Ideology: Saint Anne in Late Medieval Drama and Narrative', in Ashley and Sheingorn, *Interpreting Cultural Symbols*: pp. 111–30, p. 119.
9. See Sigmund Freud, 'The Future of an Illusion' and 'Civilization and its Discontents', in Freud, *Civilization, Society and Religion*, trans. James Strachey, ed. Albert Dickson, The Penguin Freud Library, Vol. 12 (London: Penguin, 1991): pp. 179–241 and 242–340; 'Totem and Taboo' and 'Moses and Monotheism', in Freud, *The Origins of Religion*, trans. James Strachey, ed. Albert Dickson, The Penguin Freud Library, Vol. 13 (London: Penguin, 1990): pp. 43–224 and 237–386.
10. See Freud, 'Totem and Taboo'.
11. See D. W. Winnicott, *Playing and Reality* (London: Tavistock, 1971) and *Human Nature* (London: Free Association Books, 1991).
12. 'Decree on the Invocation, Veneration and Relics of Saints and of Sacred Images', in *Dogmatic Canons and Decrees of the Council of Trent and Vatican Council I plus the Decree on the Immaculate Conception and the Syllabus of Errors of Pope Pius IX* (Rockford, IL: Tan Books, 1977): pp. 170–1.

13. 'Decree on the Invocation, Veneration and Relics', p. 171.

14. Christo Kovachevski, *The Madonna in Western Painting*, trans. Nikola Georgiev (London: Cromwell Editions, 1991), p. 31.

15. Adolfo Venturi, *The Madonna: A Pictorial Representation of the Life and Death of the Mother of Our Lord Jesus Christ by the Painters and Sculptors of Christendom in more than 500 of their Works*, trans. Alice Meynell (London: Burns & Oates, n.d.), p. 106.

The Rape of Proserpina, Bernini,
The Borghese Gallery

Apollo and Daphne, Bernini,
The Borghese Gallery

5

The Fall of Nature:
Santa Maria Maggiore and the
Villa Borghese

The story so far

The Church of Santa Maria Maggiore encapsulates the history of Catholic culture, from the conversion of Rome to the Counter-Reformation.[1] Its ancient origins evoke the goddesses of the Roman world, while its baroque art and connections with the powerful Borghese family open windows into the significance of the Counter-Reformation and its impact on the symbolic life of the Church. Its magnificent gold ceiling, said to include the first gold brought back from America by Columbus, invites reflection on the darker aspects of Christian imperialism. By allowing our imagination to wander backwards and forwards between Santa Maria Maggiore and the Villa Borghese, home to Cardinal Scipione Borghese's priceless collection of art, we can trace the changing visions and symbols that constitute the Catholic world, in order better to see how every era maps itself with particular intensity on the female body.

Legend tells that a fourth-century Roman patrician and his wife, being childless, decided to donate their wealth to the Virgin Mary and prayed to her for guidance. On the night between 4 and 5 August 358, the Madonna appeared to them in a dream and told them there would be a snowfall that night, and they should build a church to her in that place. Pope Liberius had the same dream, and the following morning the Esquiline Hill was unsea-sonably covered in snow. A church dedicated to the Virgin was built there, and for many centuries continued to be known as Sancta Maria 'ad Nives' – the Madonna of the Snow. Still today, white rose petals are showered on the altar on 5 August to symbolize the snowfall. The original church was pulled down and replaced by Pope Sixtus III in 432 to celebrate the Council of Ephesus (431), which proclaimed Mary God-bearer, *Theotokos* or *Dei Genitrix*, commonly translated as Mother of God.

The church's focus on Mary celebrates the triumph of Catholic orthodoxy over Arianism, which denied the full divinity of Christ and culminated in the Nestorian controversy. Nestorius and his followers questioned the claim that Christ was two natures – fully human and fully divine – in one person. Mary was, argued Nestorius, the mother of Christ's humanity (*Christokos*), but she was not the Mother of God (*Theotokos*). The Council of Chalce-don (451) affirmed the title *Theotokos* which was endorsed at Ephesus, marking the beginning of an era that saw the transfor-mation of the cult of Mary from its relatively sober theological and devotional origins to a celebration of the majesty of the Byzantine empire. The Mother of God thus emerged from her humble beginnings to become a queen presiding over an imperial Church, a vast maternal presence who signified Christianity's baptism or defeat of the goddess cults – depending on how one interprets it.

Santa Maria Maggiore is near the site of the temple of the Roman mother goddess, Juno Lucina, whose cult was still flour-ishing in the late Roman Empire. Juno had a particular following among pregnant Roman women, who used to invoke her protec-tion during childbirth. The 36 marble columns in Santa Maria Maggiore were part of the original church and were taken from the temple of Juno. Also dating back to the fifth century are the Old Testament mosaics above the columns and those above the altar depicting the life of the Virgin and the infancy of Christ. This ancient Christian church thus represents a space of transition from the goddess to the Madonna, and a sense of divinized maternal power shines within it. Roman women still visit the church during pregnancy, to invoke the protection of Mary in childbirth.

In the apse is a magnificent thirteenth-century mosaic in lustrous gold, red and blue, showing the coronation of the Virgin by Christ. The figures are Byzantine, but like those in Santa Maria in Trastevere, they are already acquiring the more lifelike contours and depth of later art. The mosaic emanates a sense of majesty and compassion, of divine power and human vulnerability. Christ is wearing sandals, reminding us that the King of Heaven was born of the Virgin and walked the earth as one of us. To stand beneath that cupola and gaze up at its mosaic is to sense the marriage of heaven and earth in the union between Christ and Mary. The serenity of the image enlarges rather than diminishes the onlooker, and draws us into a mysterious encounter with God in humanity and humanity in God. Alice Meynell writes, 'The mosaic ... showing us the maternal figure as something pontifical, transcends the idea of a woman. If the paradox might be permitted, one might say that although a mother is the most womanly of women, this Mother is maternal, not womanly.'[2]

It is worth noting that even today, Mary's significance in the Eastern Church is maternal rather than feminine. As the mother of Christ, she is the one in whom God became human, and it is the divinization of all humanity that is exalted in Mary. The fact that she is a woman is incidental to the glory that surrounds her as the Mother of God.

Sarah Jane Boss contrasts medieval representations of the Virgin in Majesty with modern pornography. She argues that the pornographic abuse of the human body is symptomatic of a culture of domination, which has lost a sense of the sacred in nature. The Virgin in Majesty represents the sanctification of the material world in the incarnation, and her enthronement as Queen of Heaven symbolizes 'an elegant movement of reflection and reciprocity'.[3] Such images suggest the 'willingness of the spirit to be united with matter, the potential of matter to receive the spirit, and the bonding of divinity with the physical creation'.[4] Quoting Susan Griffin, Boss argues that 'where the Virgin in Majesty is intended to instil in the devotee a sense of the sacred, the pornographic image is concerned with its denial.... Pornography silences the idea that "culture might mediate nature's power for us, and might make of our own minds and bodies the sacred vessels which transform experience into meaning."'[5]

Modern Marian art is not, in Boss's view, immune from this desecration of nature and the body. Observing the fact that modern viewers tend to be more comfortable with images that show Mary as 'meek and unassuming'[6] than with images that identify her too closely with the awesome power of nature, Boss suggests,

If the Virgin in Majesty truly does convey to the viewer a sense of divinity in the physical world, then it is worth considering that modern reaction against such an image may in part be a reaction against this central meaning. If pornography distinctly opposes the unity of spirit and matter, modern Marian iconography merely avoids any allusion to it. But that avoidance, like pornography's opposition, may be born of modernity's fear of 'nature's' power.[7]

Meynell and Boss, interestingly both English women converts to Catholicism although separated by a century in time, detect a hidden ideology at work in modern images of Mary that militates against the female body. Meynell names the two major heresies of the modern world as 'the assertion of pride' and 'the denial of compassion', and she sees both of these reflected in modern Marian art. Writing in the late nineteenth century, she witheringly refers to 'a general continental toy-shop' which has produced 'a Madonna below any kind of art – ... a doll'.[8]

From humility to humiliation

The mosaic in Santa Maria Maggiore calls to mind an era when Christianity saw in the incarnation both the humility and the holiness of the body and nature in relation to God. Today, in a world without God, humility yields to humiliation. The body in the public gaze is no longer an enigmatic invitation into mystery, but a commercial *tabula rasa* bearing the imprint of a million advertising slogans with all their implicit messages of seduction and aggression.

When did Catholic Christianity lose its holistic vision of the dignity and grace of the body redeemed in Christ? There was a gradual and uneven process of change in Christian art, from the iconic majesty of the early Middle Ages to the humanism of the Renaissance, but between the mosaic of the Virgin in Majesty and the baroque excess of the Borghese Chapel in Santa Maria Maggiore – reputedly the richest private chapel in Rome – the Catholic imagination has mutated almost beyond recognition. Baroque art and architecture is an aggressive reassertion of Catholic power in defiance of the Reformation, and a capitulation to a new form of consciousness in which man [*sic*] not God, is the source of artistic inspiration and creativity. No longer concerned with the prayerful contemplation of God in the material world, it is an hubristic assertion of the wealth and power of its patrons. The aesthetic perfection of the human body triumphs over its holy humility in the presence of God, so that paganism enjoys a brief revival of all its heroic and seductive beauty, before mutating into the romanticism and sentimentality of nineteenth- and twentieth-century religious art criticized by Meynell and Boss.

If, in the early and medieval Marian tradition, there was a period when the maternal divine power of the pagan world was harnessed and incorporated into the Christian story in a way that affirmed the redemptive significance of female society and the female body, in the seventeenth century the perspective changes. The female form is no longer a medium for the divine, but an object positioned by and subservient to the male erotic gaze. The art historian Kenneth Clark describes a transition in art from the naked body to the nude, which he associates with the refinement of artistic technique.[9] However, the feminist art historian Margaret Miles argues that in medieval representations of Eve, nakedness has religious associations that suggest the body's innocence and its vulnerability, whereas the nude represents the development of a more objectifying vision of the female body by male artists.[10] This privileging of the visual power of the aesthetic and the erotic is sometimes referred to as 'scopophilia'. To trace the beginnings of the shift from the sanctifying gaze of the religious imagination to the scopophiliac representation of the objectified and desanctified flesh, it is worth considering in more detail the baroque art of the Counter-Reformation in the context of changing attitudes towards nature, femininity and the material world.

Dis-graced nature

By the seventeenth century, the Western view of creation had become dis-graced. The combined forces of the Reformation, with its emphasis on the total corruption of nature and the power of the Word of God over the material world, and the emergence of an increasingly rationalist and scientific world-view stripped the natural order of its sacred power and inherent grace. Faced with the onslaught of Protestantism and science, the Catholic Church developed what from this distance looks like an extreme form of collective schizophrenia: on the one hand, it succumbed to the most narrow and rigid authoritarianism in its morality and doctrine, a trend that prevailed until the Second Vatican Council, and on the other hand it unleashed a repressed pagan imagination in its artists and patrons which has left its mark across the face of Rome.

Jean Bethke Elshtain argues that, with the transition from the Holy Mother Church of the medieval world to a more nationalistic and militant form of Christianity, 'A more stern and forbidding image of the patriarchal God emerged.'[11] The ecclesiastical historian Diarmaid MacCulloch writes that in the two centuries following the Reformation: 'The agendas of both Catholic and Protestant clergy and the problems facing them were surprisingly similar: they wanted to bring order and discipline to a population which was perpetually resentful of the attempt and which took a lot of taming.'[12] He goes on to observe that

> One of the oddest ways in which there was a common experience across the religious divide of the Reformation was in the obsessive fear of witches which affected Catholic and Protestant alike. There has been no complete explanation for this fear, which resulted in the deaths of thousands of people between about 1550 and 1650, on a scale which had no precedent in the medieval world.[13]

Feminist historians would not share MacCulloch's perplexity. Many would argue that there is a connection between the emergence of a more patriarchal understanding of God, the increasing social emphasis on masculine values of order and control, and the violence of the witch-hunts.

The witch-hunts began in the latter days of medieval Catholicism, when the notorious *Malleus Maleficarum* (Hammer of the Witches), a treatise written by two Dominicans and published in 1486, identified many women's traditional practices of healing and magic with witchcraft and devil-worship. However, they reached their peak during the seventeenth century, inspired by a worldview that was becoming increasingly hostile to the intuitive and non-rational dimensions of faith associated with women. The feminist historians Bonnie Anderson and Judith Zinsser describe the courts during witches' trials as 'places of extraordinary contradictions with the rational and the irrational jumbled together'.[14] (Arthur Miller's play, *The Crucible*, explores these contradictions in its dramatization of the Salem witch-hunts.)

The religious and secular authorities devised elaborate forms of torture during which they asked women pornographic questions about the experience of intercourse with the Devil. Interestingly, while Mary had been revered during the Middle Ages for her power to protect people from the devil, after the Reformation devotion to Mary became associated with superstitious and demonic practices both among Protestants and among some intellectual Catholics, so that this too sometimes became a cause for persecution and accusations of witchcraft. Thus women's religious practices with their healing powers and magical properties underwent a final purge, and Mary at last became the perfect symbol of the docile handmaid of the Almighty Father God and his henchmen on earth, while Eve was cast ever further into the outer darkness with her rebellious and headstrong daughters.

Only women who agreed to repress their womanly power and wisdom beneath deep layers of obedience, passivity and conformity would survive in such a world. However, their enemy was not reason itself, but a barely disguised pagan violence lurking just beneath the skin of the new men of religion and science. For if much medieval art is suggestive of maternal pagan power baptized in Christ, the art of the seventeenth century appeals to a different form of paganism – that of the violent male gods of the pre-Christian world, who seem to have triumphed over the incarnate compassion of the Christian God.

The pagan Church

The baroque art of the seventeenth century represents a quest for a new golden age, which looked not to the medieval world but to the ancient worlds of Greece and Rome for its inspiration, bringing their heroes and gods to life anew under the craftsmanship of the church's artists and architects. In Rome, this reached its apotheosis in the work of the sculptor and painter Gian Lorenzo Bernini (1598–1680). Besides the Colonnade in St Peter's Square, Bernini was responsible for many of the city's most lavish and ornate adornments, from the five-storey bronze canopy in the dome of St Peter's to the Fountain of the Four Rivers in the Piazza Navona. Here, one can enjoy an over-priced pizza and a glass of wine in the shadow of the vast recumbent gods of Greece – virile, muscular, their naked bodies rippling with masculine power.

But a woman might find it more revealing to visit the Borghese Gallery, built in 1613 as a sumptuous villa for Cardinal Scipione Borghese, nephew of Pope Paul V (1552–1621).[15] Paul V was responsible for enforcing the reforms of the Council of Trent and for censuring Galileo. He oversaw the completion of St Peter's Basilica, which bears his name on its entablature. Cardinal Scipione did not hesitate to use his uncle's papal influence to acquire – by fair means or foul – a priceless collection of art and sculpture both ancient and contemporary, much of which is still housed in the villa amidst rolling acres of parkland and gardens in the north of the city. In 1902 King Umberto I purchased the buildings, the park and the art collection for the state, and today they are a tranquil oasis for those seeking respite from the bustle and heat of the city.

Scipione's insatiable appetite for variety and novelty transgressed the boundaries between the sacred and profane, and his collection appropriately includes Titian's well-known painting of *Sacred and Profane Love.* In the development of the humanist vision reflected in many of the paintings in the gallery, grace and beauty were no longer the sacred preserve of religious art, for all representations of the human could theoretically reflect the beauty and nobility of the divine. But paradoxically, this transition from the symbolism of sacred art to the realism of profane art did not result in the sanctification of the profane but in the profanation of the sacred. No longer restrained by the need to communicate the mystery and potency of the divine in the context of a collective Christian vision, art became increasingly more individualistic and expressive of the fantasies, desires and projections of the artists and their patrons. The result was a sublime achievement in terms of the aesthetic, but it also signalled a decline in the transcendence, spirituality and shared symbolic significance of art, and this has particular significance for the representation of the female body. Transported from the shared domain and benefaction of religious communities into the exclusively male domain of the art academies and their patrons, the artistic imagination becomes ever more narrowly focused on the scopophilia of the male gaze.

The Villa Borghese is home to Domenichino's vast canvas of *Diana Hunting,* a work commissioned by another cardinal, Pietro Aldobrandini, but which Scipione acquired by imprisoning the artist until he reneged on the earlier commission. The painting is rich in irony, both intentional and unintentional. As Diana and her semi-naked nymphs sport in the fields and bathe in a lake, they are spied upon by two youths hiding in a bush. Mythology has it that any man viewing such a scene is cursed. At the same time, one of the nymphs lies naked in the water, legs apart, gazing straight at the viewer who is, by implication, also a male voyeur and subject to the same fate. It is in many ways a delightful painting – humorous, erotic, and one could even argue that it represents a mythical religious domain from which men are banished. But the female bodies in this painting are positioned and draped for men's arousal, and their purpose is not a celebration of women's religious power but the titillation of male onlookers, both those hidden within the painting itself, and those who stand in front of it.

If we want to contemplate the relationship between women and the divine in seventeenth-century culture, we should stand for a while before two of Bernini's magnificent works in the Borghese sculpture gallery, *Apollo and Daphne* (1625), and the *Rape of Proserpina* (1622–5). They are works of supreme artistic achievement, their white marble figures captured in a timeless moment of crisis, fear and impending catastrophe. But what do they tell us about the underlying assumptions, beliefs and values of Bernini's culture?

Apollo is the Greek god of order, harmony and civilization, the aesthetic perfection of the masculine form, and the opposite of Dionysius, the wild god of wine and women. The myth describes how one day Apollo rebuked Eros for playing with arrows, upon which the offended Eros took two arrows from his quiver and shot them from his bow. One, the arrow of love, struck Apollo. The other, the arrow of dislike, struck the nymph Daphne, daughter of the river-god Peneus. Apollo immediately fell in love with Daphne and pursued her as she ran away, desperately trying to escape his advances. Finally, losing ground and collapsing from exhaustion, she implored her father to help her. As the god took hold of her, Peneus changed her into a laurel tree. Apollo declared that as he could not possess her as a woman he would possess her as a tree instead, and henceforth those who conquered in his name would be crowned with laurel leaves.

Bernini's sculpture shows the moment of Daphne's metamorphosis. Her body is transfixed, turned away from Apollo, already turning into a woody trunk. Her arms are raised in desperation, hands and wrists mutating into branches and leaves, feet frozen in flight, long roots growing from her toes to hold her forever in the same spot. Her head is half-turned towards the god, mouth open in terror, gaze straining sideways to catch sight of him. Apollo's arm curls around her thigh and his hand presses into the perfect marble of her naked belly. He too is open-mouthed and shocked, poised in pursuit, eyes with an expression caught between longing and fear.

According to the website of the Borghese Gallery, 'The presence of this pagan myth in the Cardinal's villa was justified by a moral couplet composed in Latin by Cardinal Maffeo Barberini (later Pope Urban VIII) and engraved on the cartouche on the base, which says: *Those who love to pursue fleeting forms of pleasure, in the end find only leaves and bitter berries in their hands.*'[16]

It seems likely that the point of this epithet was lost on Scipione with his voracious appetite for accumulating material possessions. But this work of art brings home the extent to which the female body became the vehicle for all the fears and fantasies of the male spirit. Thus Daphne bears the same associations as Eve – naked female flesh representing a seductive distraction, which brings deception and disillusionment to the male who falls prey to her beauty. But what spiritual message does this work of art convey to women? How can a woman take to heart the moral message that her own flesh, hunted down and forever deprived of its human form, is a spiritual caution against 'fleeting forms of pleasure'?

Perhaps it is the greatness of Bernini's art that alternative readings are possible, if one looks beyond the immediate meanings to some deeper level of insight. Or perhaps it is just that, if a woman is to permit herself the pleasure of much Western art, she must develop an oblique and subversive vision. This entails a creative struggle to liberate female sexuality from the compulsive violence of the pornographic gaze, by looking anew at our symbolic and artistic inheritance. Censorship seeks to deny and exclude that which it finds unpalatable about the creative imagination. It is a more difficult but ultimately more liberating task to cultivate a vision that is not only unafraid of what it sees, but that can somehow redeem the beauty, the fragility and the inevitable partiality of any act of human creativity, and incorporate it into the redemptive hope of humankind, which is both revealed and concealed in the genius of Christian art.

Trapped between Apollo's desire and Peneus's fatherly intervention, Daphne faces an impossible choice – to retain her place in culture and her human identity by succumbing to the demands of the man who would possess her, or to buy her freedom at the terrible cost of her exile from culture into a state of nature. Does Daphne know the impossibility of her choice? Does Bernini unwittingly show us that moment of realization which was played out every time a woman refused to succumb to the authority of men and found herself tied to a stake and her limbs consumed by flames? Bernini's Daphne symbolizes the metamorphosis that the idea of woman underwent at the beginning of the modern age, reflecting wider philosophical and religious transformations. Half-body, half-tree, thwarting and frustrating the desire of the male god but at the same time forever falling under his control, she tells us much about the relationship between man, woman, divinity and nature that emerged in European consciousness in the seventeenth century and still holds us in its grip.

But is she not also a monument to women's resistance? Perhaps she is a memorial to every woman who has chosen martyrdom rather than submission, or who has experienced cultural exclusion as the consequence of refusing to conform to the demands of a society that would deprive her of her integrity, her freedom and her right to choose. Bernini's Daphne shows us the cost to women of inhabiting a world in which the only choices we have are between a state of culture dominated by men and a state of nature identified with women. Better to flourish as an evergreen tree, says Daphne, rooted in the earth, sign of mute protest, than to bow down before this despised god. How many women made the same choice in the Early Church, preferring martyrdom and freedom to enslavement and idolatry? How many women today, faced with the idolatrous masculinity of the Church's idea of God, choose exile over conformity, secularized materialism over a Christian culture of male domination? Better perhaps to live the vegetable existence of consumerism than to retain one's spiritual life through the worship of a male god intent on possessing and controlling the female flesh.

No less brilliant in its mastery, even more disturbing in its imagery, is Bernini's *Rape of Proserpina* – daughter of Gaia, a Roman version of the Greek myth of Demeter and Persephone. Again, we have a young girl caught in flight by a male god. Again, there is the same anguished terror on her face, the same open mouth and arms upraised, this time as if to ward off her attacker. Tears trickle down her marble cheeks, and she brings her knees up as if to protect herself from the rape that is to come. Unlike the youthful and beautiful Apollo, Pluto is strong and muscular, with a wild beard and a mouth spread in a lascivious grin, eyes fixed leeringly on his prey. He grasps Proserpina against his naked torso, fingers digging into the flesh of her belly and thigh. Her legs and feet flail helplessly in the air, and beneath her sits the three-headed dog that guards Hades, snarling savagely up at her.

I have described how feminist interpreters see the myth of Demeter and Persephone as symbolizing a time of transition between maternal and paternal religious cults. It is perhaps not surprising that this myth re-emerges at a time when the maternal feminine dimension of the story of God incarnate is being eclipsed by a more violent and patriarchal concept of God. Nevertheless, as with the Daphne sculpture, Bernini's Proserpina can be liberated from her captivity to the eroticized male gaze and become a symbol that speaks to and with women.

Look again at Proserpina, and see the victim of rape. Look at the tears so delicately carved on her cheek. Feel the cruelty of Pluto's grip on her flesh. Look at her resistance, and the despair on her face. This is not a woman who means yes when she says no. She is not 'asking for it'. She gazes imploringly towards the onlooker, perhaps searching for her mother amidst the faces of the cardinals and patrons who leer and fantasize before her. Look at Proserpina, and share her howl of anguish and outrage at the violence that men do to women. Look at Pluto and see the raw brutality of pagan power when it is divinized and unleashed in the dark underworld of men's fantasies. See his face close to, as Proserpina does. Sense the rank heat of his sweat and his breath, and hear the possessive rasp of his voice. Hear too the snarl of the dog and see its bared fangs. Wait for the tearing apart of vulnerable flesh that is about to happen.

A male journalist, writing recently about Bernini, is less critical in his description. Referring to Bernini's power 'to set pulses racing', he goes on to say that *The Rape of Proserpina*, 'in which Pluto carries off his bride in manly triumph – is a mass of thighs and haunches, as is his *Apollo and Daphne'*.[17]

Daphne and Proserpina are images from a world in which both God and woman had become projections of man – the powerful, virile male God, and the captive, conquered woman. It is perhaps no less telling to visit Bernini's *Ecstasy of St Teresa* (1644) in the Church of Santa Maria della Vittoria. The work is inspired by a passage in Teresa's autobiography, when she describes a rapturous experience in which an angel seemed to be plunging an arrow tipped with fire again and again into her body. In Bernini's statue, Teresa reclines in ecstatic abandonment with her head thrown back, her eyes rolling and her mouth half-open, while an angel stands beside her with a flaming arrow. Jacques Lacan, exploring what he sees as the relationship between female mysticism and sexual ecstasy (*jouissance*), says of this work, 'Just go look at Bernini's statue in Rome, you'll see right away that St Teresa is coming, there's no doubt about it.'[18] To this, Irigaray ironically replies, 'In Rome? So far away? To look? At a statue? Of a saint? Sculpted by a man? What pleasure are we talking about? Whose pleasure?'[19]

There is a strong resemblance between Bernini's Daphne, Proserpina and Teresa. All three are caught in a moment of sexual encounter with a male god, and if Teresa's experience is one of ecstasy rather than terror, this is communicated only by the most subtle difference. Seen exclusively from the perspective of the masculine imagination, Christian spirituality has taken on the contours of women's sexual ravishment by a male god. One might think of John Donne, writing in the same century, imploring God to

> Take mee to you, imprison mee, for I
> Except you'enthrall mee, never shall be free,
> Nor ever chast, except you ravish mee.

Even as it sought to purge itself of the rich maternal fecundity of the Middle Ages, the seventeenth century was projecting a different kind of carnal significance onto the female flesh. The control and subjugation of female sexuality by male power – the power of reason or the power of God – became one of the driving impulses of science and religion. And this affected not only the representation of women but also the representation of nature itself.

Feminine nature and masculine science

With a rationalized and dematerialized God came a rationalized and dematerialized man. No longer did humankind belong among the species and functions of nature, albeit with a capacity for transcendence and reason that made humanity unique in the natural world. Now, man was enthroned as lord over all, and the material world had become a mechanism and a resource to be exploited by human industry. If this was primarily a revolution in Protestant thought, the Catholic Church had lost the robust earthiness of medieval religion and become a more inward-looking and defensive institution. In the grip of its own bureaucratic and authoritarian reforms, it was hardly in a position to challenge the single-minded pursuit of science and reason that was emerging as the motivating force in Western thought. With determination, discipline and perseverance, everything could be made subject to the laws of reason – even God – and the man of knowledge could become the master of the universe.

Yet nature was not and is not totally within human control, so even as the rationalizing mind sought increasing domination over nature, the men of science still encountered aspects of nature that seemed endowed with a mysterious and threatening power. The result was that nature was not only rationalized, it was also sexualized. If on the one hand it was raw material to be used and exploited by men, on the other hand it was a capricious and unpredictable body, which became endowed with the attributes of wanton female sexuality. Henceforth both nature and women must be penetrated and interrogated in order to render them compliant and submissive to the demands of science.

Francis Bacon (1561–1626), philosopher, man of law and scientist, epitomizes this intellectual revolution. Carolyn Merchant, in her book *The Death of Nature*, says of Bacon that he 'fashioned a new ethic sanctioning the exploitation of nature'.[20] Referring to Bacon's book *The Masculine Birth of Time*, Merchant writes that 'Although a female's inquisitiveness may have caused man's fall from his God-given dominion, the relentless interrogation of another female, nature, could be used to regain it.'[21] Bacon made explicit the association between the investigation of nature and the interrogation of witches. He writes, 'For you have but to follow and as it were hound nature in her wanderings, and you will be able when you like to lead and drive her afterward to the same place again.' Relating this to the witch trials, he goes on to say of these that 'a useful light may be gained, not only for a true judgment of the offenses of persons charged with such practices, but likewise for the further disclosing of the secrets of nature. Neither ought a man to make scruple of entering and penetrating into these holes and corners, when the inquisition of truth is his whole object…'[22] Merchant points out the implications of this sexual metaphor, given that the witch trials often involved gynaecological examinations looking for evidence that the accused had had sex with the devil.

But metaphors of penetration are also bound up with the emergence of a new economic order in which mining, particularly mining for gold in the newly colonized territories of the East Indies and South America, was becoming a lucrative commercial venture. The ceiling in Santa Maria Maggiore is said to be gilded with the first gold Christopher Columbus brought back from the New World, given as a gift by Queen Isabella to the Pope. Bridging the space between the Coronation of the Virgin and the Borghese Chapel, it suggests the cost of Christian Europe's transition from medieval Christendom to global empire.

Merchant argues that, until the sixteenth century, there were ethical constraints against mining the body of Mother Earth. Quoting ancient Roman and Greek writers, she demonstrates a persistent resistance to mining running through Western attitudes to nature, so that even in the Renaissance the human and natural worlds were seen to be in an I–thou relationship, in which 'nature was considered to be a person-writ-large'.[23] But when European expansionism opened up territories with mines ripe for exploitation, a new ethos began to emerge: 'One does not readily slay a mother, dig into her entrails for gold or mutilate her body, although commercial mining would soon require that.'[24] 1556 saw the publication of Georg Agricola's treatise on mining, *De Re Metallica*, in which he refuted the ancient appeals to the sanctity of Mother Earth and offered the first modern justification for mining as a commercial activity. To return to Donne's poetry, by the time he was writing in the early seventeenth century, the imagery of mining in the New World had become a metaphor for seducing his mistress:

> License my roaving hands, and let them go,
> Before, behind, between, above, below.
> O my America! my new-found-land,
> My kingdome, safeliest when with one man man'd
> My mynne of precious stones, My Emperie,
> How blest am I in this discovering thee!

Nature as Eve

The idea of probing the female body as a metaphor for scientific knowledge and the control of nature had as its dark and irrational underside the ancient fear of female sexuality, encoded within the Western masculine imaginary primarily through the association of Eve with temptation, seduction and death. But until the sixteenth century, it was Mary, not Eve, who was identified with nature, for in the flesh of Mary the whole natural world had been redeemed in Christ. Anselm, writing in the twelfth century, expresses early and medieval Christian attitudes when he refers to Mary as 'virgin blessed and ever blessed, whose blessing is upon all nature'.[25]

But by the seventeenth century, Mary had been all but eradicated from Protestant consciousness, and she had become dissociated from nature and the body in the Catholic imagination. In the scientific revolution, all the attributes that had once been associated with Eve were projected onto a natural world divested of its redemptive maternal power. Like Eve, nature had become the enemy rather than the nurturing mother of human culture and creativity. Freud, self-professed man of reason, science and secularism, writes that 'the principal task of civilization ... is to defend us against nature'. He goes on, 'But no one is under the illusion that nature has already been vanquished; and few dare to hope that she will ever be entirely subject to man.... Nature rises up against us, majestic, cruel and inexorable; she brings to our mind once more our weakness and helplessness, which we thought to escape through the work of civilization.'[26]

In one form or another, in the long development of Western culture and consciousness, from the origins of Christianity to the science and technology of postmodernity, the female body has haunted the project of civilization. Neither inside nor outside the story of salvation in its religious and scientific versions, Eve is the other – nature, the body, woman – who still taunts and seduces the sons of Adam.

To stand as Eve beneath the gold ceiling of Santa Maria Maggiore is to stand in the place of the silenced other, the sexual female body, the natural world, and to acquire the knowledge that comes through exclusion and non-being. It is to agree to the loss of innocence that comes with the knowledge of evil. It is to refuse the undemanding beauty of the aesthetic, by knowing the wrong that it hides.

How then might we begin to gather up these broken threads of the past, acknowledging all the contradictions and complexities of the Christian legacy at the beginning of the third millennium? Is it possible to weave them into a narrative of memory and anticipation, of repentance and hope, which opens up the story of the Church to a new and unpredictable future?

In the slow and imaginative task of cultivating hope, we need to weave liturgical as well as theological, political and sexual visions of past and future possibilities. This means attending to that pivotal point at the heart of the Catholic faith, which is the Mass. Like everything else, this too is shaped by the world in which it belongs, and yet it beckons us into a space of mystery which is God's invitation to humankind. So let us go now to St Peter's Square and join the crowds who have gathered from all over the world, to mourn the failures and lost opportunities of the past, and to nurture the hopes and promises of the future that opens ahead of us.

Notes

1. See Josef Pustka, *The Basilica of Santa Maria Maggiore* (Rome: D.EDI.T.s.r.l., 1997).
2. Meynell, *Mary, the Mother of Jesus*, p. 72.
3. See Sarah Jane Boss, *Empress and Handmaid: On Nature and Gender in the Cult of the Virgin Mary* (London and New York: Cassell, 2000), p. 4.
4. Ibid.
5. Ibid., p. 3, quoting Susan Griffin, *Pornography and Silence* (London: Women's Press, 1981), p. 71.
6. Ibid., p. 9.
7. Ibid.

8. Meynell, *Mary, the Mother of Jesus*, p. 85.

9. See Kenneth Clark, *The Nude: A Study in Ideal Art* (London: John Murray, 1956).

10. See Margaret Miles, *Carnal Knowing: Female Nakedness and Religious Meaning in the Christian West* (Tunbridge Wells: Burns & Oates, 1992), pp. 12–16.

11. Jean Bethke Elshtain, *Public Man, Private Woman: Women in Social and Political Thought* (Princeton, NJ: Princeton University Press, 1993), p. 105.

12. Diarmaid MacCulloch, *Groundwork of Christian History* (London: Epworth Press, 1987), p. 195.

13. Ibid.

14. Bonnie S. Anderson and Judith P. Zinsser, *A History of their Own: Women in Europe from Prehistory to the Present*, Vol. I (London: Penguin, 1988), p. 169.

15. See Paolo Moreno and Chiara Stefani, *The Borghese Gallery* (Milan: Touring Club Italiano, 2000).

16. Website of Borghese Gallery, *www.galleriaborghese.it/default-en.htm*.

17. Richard Owen, 'Art Lovers Practise the Art of Love', *The Times*, 11 June 2001.

18. See Jacques Lacan, 'God and the *Jouissance* of the Woman', in Juliet Mitchell and Jacqueline Rose (eds), *Feminine Sexuality: Jacques Lacan and the Ecole Freudienne*, trans. Jacqueline Rose (Basingstoke: Macmillan, 1982): pp. 137–48.

19. Luce Irigaray, *This Sex Which is Not One*, trans. Catherine Porter with Carolyn Burke (Ithaca, NY: Cornell University Press, 1985), pp. 90–1.

20. Carolyn Merchant, *The Death of Nature: Women, Ecology and the Scientific Revolution* (San Francisco, CA: Harper & Row, 1979), p. 164.

21. Ibid., p. 170.

22. Francis Bacon, quoted in ibid., p. 168.

23. Ibid., p. 28.

24. Ibid., p. 3.

25. Anselm, *The Prayers and Meditations of Saint Anselm with the Proslogion*, trans. Sister Benedicta Ward, SLG (London: Penguin, 1973), p. 120.

26. Sigmund Freud, 'The Future of an Illusion', in Freud, *Civilization, Society and Religion* (Harmondsworth: Penguin, 1985): p. 195.

The Ecstacy of St Teresa, Bernini, Church of Santa Maria della Vittoria

Mass at St Peter's

6

Dancing in the Dark:
Mass at St Peter's

The broken Church

Without beauty, without majesty (we saw him),
no looks to attract our eyes;
a thing despised and rejected by men,
a man of sorrows and familiar with suffering,
a man to make people screen their faces;
he was despised and we took no account of him.

The American nun is reading from Isaiah 53. Her voice rings out over the heads of the crowds assembled for Sunday Mass in St Peter's Square, gathered inside the encircling arms of Bernini's colonnade. Michelangelo's dome looms in front of us: an imposing assertion of Rome's enduring power. The jubilee crowds are brightly dressed in summer clothes, bringing a carnivalesque atmosphere to the solemn proceedings of the papal Mass. People of every nationality and of many different creeds have been brought together not only by the tourist attractions of Rome but also by the charismatic appeal of Pope John Paul II. A trio of Hare Krishna men slouches past, and a cluster of Japanese women huddles together in the shade of an umbrella. Somewhere nearby a mobile phone bleeps impatiently.

In front of the altar on the steps of the basilica, a small green figure slumps over his bishop's crook. The television cameras zoom in, and the screens erected for our benefit show us a face that is weary and etched in pain, eyes closed, mouth slack. A man of sorrows and familiar with suffering. We are privy to a ritual that is the opposite of the celebrity gaze normally afforded by television cameras. Instead of avoiding the stricken face of the Pope, the cameras linger on it, magnify it, confronting us with some mysterious challenge. Without beauty, without majesty. An exhausted and sick old man, huddled beneath the imperial majesty and beauty of Rome, bearing the weight of the Church on his back. A man to make people screen their faces.

In the glare of the sunshine and the murmur of the crowds, the Mass becomes a crucible in which all the madness and holiness, all the power and vulnerability, all the disgrace and glory of the Catholic faith are gathered together. This is a broken Church in a broken world, without beauty, without majesty, yet encountering God in the broken moment, in the broken language, in the broken bread and the broken body of the Eucharist. The magnificence and depravity of art. The grandeur and corruption of human endeavour. The tragedy and comedy of history. The pathos and promise of our dreams and visions. The liturgy of the Mass gathers everything in, consecrates it, and offers the broken body of history and culture to its creator and redeemer. The words of a modern hymn by Kevin Nichols express this reconciliation between human endeavour and divine grace:

> In bread we bring you, Lord,
>   our bodies' labour.
> In wine we offer you
>   our spirits' grief....
> Take all that daily toil
>   plants in our hearts' poor soil,
> take all we start and spoil,

each hopeful dream,
the chances we have missed,
the graces we resist,
Lord, in thy Eucharist,
take and redeem.

Christian history can be seen as a sorry catalogue of missed chances and resisted graces, but that is too narrow an interpretation, for the Christian story also lays before us the genius of human creativity and love's capacity to rise again and again from the ashes of violence. The story of the Church is the human story. Collectively and individually, Christians share in the world's vulnerability, ambiguity and power. An authentic quest for truth draws us into shadows where we must look carefully for glimmers of light and beauty not apart from but dancing within the darkness. Truth, like God, does not come to us pure and uncontaminated by language and life. It is veiled, enigmatic, persistent both in the claims it makes upon us and in its power to elude us.

Modern historians, psychologists and cultural theorists have shown us that every human story, whether of an individual life, of a family, of a nation, or of a religious tradition, is a multiplicity of sometimes competing and conflicting identities and voices, each of which has some claim to truth and authenticity, even when those claims appear to contradict and cancel each other out. In Rome, history gives the mistaken impression of unfolding in a smooth progression of succeeding narratives from Greek to Roman to Christian empires and then to modernity. The traumas and disruptions of history have interrupted but not broken its continuities. But if we compare this with that other holy city – Jerusalem – then we realize that there is never one truth about the world. I visited Israel with a group of Orthodox Jews during the Christian Holy Week several years ago. While pilgrim

Christians prayed and preached and prepared to celebrate Easter, our group was being shown the Holy Land through Jewish eyes. A third story – the Muslim story of Israel – was a persistent, palpable presence, even although it was never alluded to. The Dome of the Rock in Jerusalem bears within itself this history of fragmentation, disruption and conflict, having been the site of a Jewish temple, a Christian church, a mosque, a crusader church, and now a mosque again. If Rome creates the illusion of a triumphant and homogenous world-view, Jerusalem is a reminder that humankind is still caught up in the anguished process of creating the story of God in the world out of a multiplicity of competing narratives.

To appreciate this complexity without imposing upon it a logic of right and wrong, of winners and losers, is to strive for a vision that takes us beyond the morality of the Fall – the enslaving morality of a dualistic world in which the knowledge of good and evil sows seeds of violence and persecution in the human heart. It reminds us that even as we struggle for justice, truth and meaning, we ourselves are implicated and entangled in the injustice and violence of life. Authenticity lies not in pretending that we can extricate ourselves from the web of belonging and becoming with all its compromises and negotiations, but in being honest with and about ourselves and the world.

Human misery and God's mercy

It is the costly process of repentance and forgiveness that smoothes the jagged edge of history and gives hope to those who have been silenced, exploited and oppressed. It is not within our human power either to seek or grant forgiveness on behalf of the dead, but we can seek God's forgiveness in the midst of the living, and therefore the narrative of human forgiveness has to be rooted in a narrative of God's forgiveness. Christianity lays before us the ultimate victim of violence, who is the love of God incarnate on the cross. By refusing to flinch from that deepest and most profound exposure of the wounds humankind inflicts on the body of love, we pray for healing and redemption by those wounds, even though we know that we too inflict them again and again by the wilful or careless neglects of daily life.

So we begin our worship with an act of repentance, a moment of truthfulness when we recognize that the grace of God's presence is not dependent upon the morality or success of our lives. God asks only that we come into the divine presence in spirit and in truth. That is surely what repentance is. It sets aside the need to pretend, and allows us to make peace with ourselves, with one another, and with God:

I confess to Almighty God and to you, my brothers and sisters,
that I have sinned through my own fault
in my thoughts and in my words,
in what I have done,
and in what I have failed to do.

Catherine of Siena claims that the only unforgivable sin is that of the soul who in the end believes that her misery is greater than God's mercy. The failure to accept God's forgiveness is the ultimate act of pride and defiance against God, one which perhaps even God cannot overcome. It is mercy, not misery, that gives birth to the future in time as well as in eternity, and frees us from the past so that we can greet the future with hope.

The purpose of an examination of conscience is not to punish ourselves, but to find liberation from the unexamined ghosts that haunt us and hold us. In the biblical story of the Samaritan woman at the well (John 4:1–42), Jesus confronts the woman with the truth about her life, not in order to shame her but in order to free her. His acceptance of her is based not on pretence but on the person she really is. He knows that she has had five husbands and that the man she now lives with is not her husband. In this space of loving honesty between them, he too can reveal himself for who he is: 'I am he' (John 4:26). When a bleeding woman in the crowd surreptitiously touches the hem of his robe (Luke 8:43–48), Jesus exposes her action not to condemn her but to bring her into the light, to praise her faith, and to free her from the burden of secrecy. He shows that she has nothing to hide and nothing to be ashamed of. Contrary to what people think, contrary to what she herself might believe, her touch does not pollute him but is welcomed by him as a sign of faith. Thus Christ transforms our deepest shames and fears into the grace of forgiveness and healing. This is beautifully expressed in George Herbert's poem, 'Love':

> Love bade me welcome: yet my soul drew back,
>   Guilty of dust and sin.
> But quick-ey'd Love, observing me grow slack
>   From my first entrance in,
> Drew nearer to me, sweetly questioning,
>   If I lack'd any thing.
>
> A guest, I answer'd, worthy to be here:
>   Love said, You shall be he.
> I the unkind, ungrateful? Ah my dear,
>   I cannot look on thee.
> Love took my hand, and smiling did reply,
>   Who made the eyes but I?
>
> Truth Lord, but I have marr'd them: let my shame
>   Go where it doth deserve.
> And know you not, says Love, who bore the blame?
>   My dear, then I will serve.

You must sit down, says Love, and taste my meat:
So I did sit and eat.

So often, Christianity instils the idea of a punitive and distant God, so that we develop a sense of sin and guilt, which forms a barrier between our own tormented spirits and the healing touch of Christ. Contrary to all the images the gospels offer us of Christ's healing tenderness towards women's bodies, many Catholic women today still struggle with a sense of shame over their sexuality and bodily functions. Feminist theologians have argued that the Church's whole concept of sin needs to be revised, because it focuses too exclusively on masculine sins of pride, lust, greed and ambition. For women, they argue, sin might have more to do with excessive self-denigration and a failure to cultivate qualities of self-respect, dignity and personal responsibility. So an examination of conscience does not only mean confessing what we perceive to be wrong in ourselves. It also means examining our guilt in the light of God's love, and asking if perhaps we need healing rather than forgiveness, liberation rather than penance.

Increasingly today, there is also an awareness that sin is relational – it does not refer to the violation of abstract and absolute moral principles, but to the betrayal of love in human relationships. We are rediscovering the truth of God's words to Catherine of Siena: 'every sin committed against me is done by means of your neighbours.'[1] Some would argue that this idea of the relationality of sin is in itself one of the insights women bring to theology. If, as Gilligan and others argue,[2] women are culturally conditioned to put relationships before rules, to attend to the demands of care before the demands of moral autonomy, then we need a new understanding of sin, one which draws on the insights of psychology and the human sciences. The moral absolutes issuing from the Vatican with regard to issues of sexuality, fertility and love cannot possibly take into account the infinitely complex demands of building and sustaining relationships of loving integrity. A moral vision that concerns itself with issues of power, violence, responsibility and care in relationships between individuals, communities and nations is more viable than one based on absolute principles, and gives us greater resources to make mature moral decisions based on the demands of love and reason, commitment and integrity.

But all this means that an act of confession does not involve only God and myself. Somewhere, however distantly or implicitly, it must always involve a third party. That is one of the positive insights of the confessional: a sin against God is always a sin against the community, for we never sin in the abstract. Confession is an expression of faith in the power of God's love to mediate forgiveness between persons – the 'sinner' and the priest as representative of the wounded other, supremely embodied and wounded in Christ himself.

This means that seeking forgiveness and making peace are inseparable from the freedom that comes with absolution and forgiveness. There is cleansing anguish in going to somebody we have hurt very badly, betrayed without their knowledge perhaps, and asking forgiveness, in bringing our wrongs into the healing light. For those who cannot do that, because the wound of honesty would be too painful for the other to bear, or because there is no longer any possibility of communication, the burden of guilt and regret gnaws at the soul and becomes a form of penance almost too bitter to bear. That is when only God's forgiveness, grace beyond human understanding, might sometimes pierce the darkness and heal the grief.

If asking forgiveness is one form of liberation, offering it is another and perhaps more costly process, which we might find impossible if we have been violated or harmed beyond endurance by another's deliberate or unintentional actions. But to refuse forgiveness is to remain trapped in the hell of bitterness and vengeance. In the words of Milton's *Paradise Lost*, 'The mind is its own place, and in itself / Can make a Heav'n of Hell, a Hell of Heav'n.'

The media today bring us stories of those whose loved ones have been victims of terrible crimes – the parents of murdered children, the relatives of those who have died in acts of terrorism – and it is those who cannot forgive who remain imprisoned and tortured by the desire for retribution. It is impossible to ask or expect anyone to make that forgiving move, and unless we have been in that situation we cannot know how we ourselves might feel. But there are also those who have come to a point of acceptance and forgiveness of sorts, and they are the ones in whom we see the healing power of the desire to forgive. Marian Partington, whose beloved sister, Lucy, was tortured and murdered by Frederick and Rosemary West, has spoken of her pity for Rosemary West and the peace that she has achieved through struggling towards acceptance if not forgiveness. When the Oklahoma bomber, Timothy McVeigh, was awaiting the death-sentence, interviews with some of his victims revealed a stark difference between those who believed that the death penalty would bring 'closure', and those who recognized that it was not killing McVeigh but going beyond their own hatred and unforgiveness that would liberate them from his power over their lives. In Northern Ireland, Gordon Wilson cradled his dying daughter, Marie, in his arms after the IRA bombing at Enniskillen. He has since become a campaigner for peace and a symbol of hope for the country's divided Catholic and Protestant communities. Pope John Paul II gave the world an example of forgiveness when he visited in prison the man who had shot him.

Mary Midgeley, in her book *Wickedness*, offers an analysis of the ways in which the natural but transient hostilities that arise in human interaction can become destructive obsessions directed towards both ourselves and others. She explores the idea of evil as a negation, not a positive power in itself but a distortion of positive virtues in human relationships and behaviour. It is when our life-affirming capacities to desire what is good become perverted that we experience what Freud interpreted as the death wish and become prey to obsessions: 'Destruction, both for oneself and others, can indeed become an aim, even a dominant aim, but only through perversion, recombination and narrowing of natural desires.' Midgeley goes on to describe self-destruction as 'a secondary, but seemingly inevitable, consequence of indulged resentment'.[3] Her argument is agnostic in so far as it neither affirms nor denies the possibility of God, but her careful and thoughtful analysis can help theological reflection on human orientations towards violence and vengeance.

If we recognize that there is a close affinity between forgiving, being forgiven, and being released from the power of hatred and alienation, then perhaps we begin to understand why God's mercy and justice are not opposing forces but qualities that are intrinsic to the meaning of reconciliation, love and freedom. Justice demands retribution unless the one who has been wounded offers forgiveness, so that only mercy can set aside the need for vengeance. Thus it is the combined power of repentance and forgiveness that can free us from the spiral of vengeance and violence.

Affirming goodness

What place does God's love and forgiveness have in extreme stories of human suffering? How can we relate the destruction that explodes with such devastating power into the lives of human beings to faith in an all-powerful and all-good God who is just and loving? John Paul II asks, 'Could God have *justified Himself* before human history, so full of suffering, without placing Christ's Cross at the center of that history?'⁴

Ultimately, if God is love, then any offence against love is an offence against God, and it is the distortion of love, the obsessive refusal of love's reconciling power, that traps us in the spiral of violence. But love is costly, for faithful love is an active, truthful commitment to the well-being and flourishing of the other. It is this outward-looking orientation, this life of responsivity towards others, that frees us from being consumed by our own anxieties and vanities. Marriage and family life are a training ground for love because they teach us the cost and endeavour of loving, the demands it makes upon us by way of justice, truth, integrity and attentiveness to another's well-being. And because love is violated every day by our smallest actions of indifference and neglect, by the enormity of our potential for betrayal and destruction, only forgiveness preserves love's integrity and love's endurance. In the favourite film of my teenage years, *Love Story*, there was a famous line, 'Love means never having to say you're sorry.' When I was sixteen, I thought that was a wonderfully romantic idea. Now, I realize that 'sorry', sincerely meant and actively expressed, is the word by which we sustain and heal love. It renews love, and it is an expression of faith and trust as well as of hope. It is the word by which we acknowledge and commit ourselves to going beyond our own and the other's capacity to wound, linking together yesterday's ignorance with today's awakening and tomorrow's promise.

The cross shows us love wounded beyond endurance and love affirmed beyond death. It is God's acknowledgement that human-kind too bears the wounds of love, that in making us in God's image God made us for love's wounding. How can this be shown? How can this be offered? Come God, let us make you in our image and see you suffer as we do. Tell us you understand. Show us that you know what a parent feels like when a child is murdered. Let us see how you would feel if you were betrayed by those you trust and abandoned by your friends. Prove to us that your love would not weaken even if you were stripped, abused, tortured and humiliated because you would not meet violence with violence. Show us that you understand what it costs the human being to love. Show us that you wouldn't weaken if you had to suffer as we do. Become for us all the love and all the heartache of all the world, but more than that, become for us all the agony and all the dying of all the world. Be vulnerable, like us. And show us that love's vulnerability is greater than death's annihilating power. Show us that the forces of negation cannot quench love's presence. Let us test you to the limits of your endurance, and then we will forgive you for making us creatures in the image of your crucified love. And if you survive the test, then will you forgive us?

This is the spirit's cry when she stands before the cross, and it is a cry that must arise from every individual heart. We cannot change the world by force, nor by ideology. If the world is to change without violence, then that change must be one of personal transformation, which becomes greater than the sum of its parts when it spreads through time and space. Every human being is invited to look beyond death's negation to the image of love that is the image of God within us, the image of love incarnate in a mother's womb, the image of love crucified on the cross of history. In the inevitable confrontation with violence and hatred, each one of us must decide again and again whether to meet violence with violence or with love. And because we are not God, because our first instinct to love has often been bruised and violated by experience, we know that the violent impulse, the angry word, the hostile stare, express themselves time and again as our first response to provocation. So making peace becomes the ongoing work of every human life and of the human story from that first experience of exile from Eden to the ultimate longing for heaven's joy.

When we look back individually and collectively, we recognize that Christian love is yet to be expressed and revealed in a way that would heal the broken worlds we create for human habitation – our fragmented psyches, our tortured loves, our failed relationships, our thwarted dreams. In our own age, we also acknowledge that the very body that incarnates Christ among us – the body of the Christian Church – bears the burden of a history scarred and shattered by violence, oppression and greed. Far from being a light to the world, the Church has so often been associated with the darkest and most shameful episodes in history.

That is why it is impossible to overestimate the significance of the fact that, at the beginning of the new millennium, Pope John Paul II resisted the advice of many of the cardinals and initiated a public act of apology for the sins of Christian history. In March 2000, he led a collective liturgy of repentance on behalf of the whole Church. This was a carefully worded gesture, which maintained a distinction between the Church herself and the sinful actions of her people. Some would say that he thereby perpetuated the idea of the Church as a perfect and incorruptible presence in the world, whatever the wrongdoings of Christians themselves, a distinction between the mystical and the institutional Church, which many today find unacceptable. Others believe that the Pope's apology did not go far enough – for example, with regard to acknowledging the extent of the Church's historical abuse of women. Nevertheless, it was a symbolic gesture with vast repercussions. It was a reminder that the Church of the Counter-Reformation – defensive, other-worldly, hostile to change – has changed almost beyond recognition, a change that can be traced back to the Second Vatican Council in the early 1960s.

The Second Vatican Council

It is sometimes said that the Catholic Church thinks in centuries, suggesting that it is futile to expect her to adapt easily to changing cultural norms. But the late twentieth century was a time of dramatic transformation within the Church, and Vatican II has acted as a catalyst that has extended far beyond the institutional Church. Today, there is almost a schism between conservative and liberal Catholics, with an increasing tendency towards authoritarianism apparently threatening the reforms of the Council. But in historical terms, this was a volcanic event in Catholic consciousness, perhaps in its way as dramatic and revolutionary as the Reformation. It will take centuries to work its way through all the complex labyrinths of the global Church and to find its level in so many different cultural, economic and geographical contexts. Only the most ruthless and draconian moves would be able to halt the kaleidoscopic visions still taking shape in the aftermath of the Council, and it seems improbable that in the era of information technology and democratic ideals, the Vatican could ever again launch a counter-offensive along the lines of the Council of Trent.

It is also important to recognize that, if there has been a tendency towards authoritarianism during the papacy of John Paul II, there has been another dimension to his papacy that future generations might regard as being more significant than his failings.

It is true than in terms of the Church's moral teaching and institutional structures, John Paul II has in many ways been a reactionary force. However, his social encyclicals are among the finest social critiques to emerge from the late twentieth century, and his writings on women have also been revolutionary. This is not least because some of them – his 1988 apostolic letter, *Mulieris Dignitatem*, and his 1995 'Letter to Women' – have been addressed directly to women. *Mulieris Dignitatem*, while not being entirely free of feminine stereotypes and romantic ideals, is remarkable in its treatment of Eve as well as Mary. It reiterates themes that are found in his earlier catechesis on Genesis, *Original Unity of Man and Woman*, about the equality and mutuality of the sexes in creation, each of whom constitutes a gift of the self to the other.

Perhaps for the first time since the patristic era, in *Mulieris Dignitatem* a male theologian contemplates the story of salvation in a way that recognizes the significance of the woman, not in dualistic terms of sin and grace, temptation and obedience, but in a more subtle vision of a shared endeavour that situtates her at the centre of salvation history. Thus, in *Mulieris Dignitatem*, John Paul II describes the perfect reconciliation between Eve and Mary that is hinted at in so many patristic writings: 'The comparison Eve–Mary can be understood ... in the sense that Mary assumes in herself and embraces the mystery of the "woman" whose beginning is Eve, "the mother of all the living" (Genesis 3:20).'[5]

Related to this, and recalling my suggestion that theologians have focused on Eve's sin while overlooking Cain's sin, perhaps it is no coincidence that, in his 1995 encyclical *Evangelium Vitae*, John Paul II focuses on the murder of Abel as the originating act of violence. It is Cain's fratricide rather than Eve's temptation that now symbolizes the violent entry of death into the world, and this is played out in 'the culture of death' that constitutes the modern world order. The man and woman prove vulnerable to evil in Paradise, but it is in the story of Cain and Abel that this evil begins to manifest itself in the form of violent death.[6]

So whatever the difficulties and obstacles that must inevitably arise at times of great change, the late twentieth century marks a turning point in Eve's story and in the story of the relationship between woman, man, God, the Church and the world. The Second Vatican Council, the rise of feminist consciousness, and the papacy of John Paul II, are not mutually opposing forces. They are shared and hopeful visions emerging from the injustices and silences of history, and we should not be surprised that their birth is marked by pain and struggle.

The reforms of the Council manifest themselves at every level of Church life. An American woman reading the Bible in English at the papal Mass in front of a multicultural throng is a potent symbol of this. The translation of the liturgy from Latin into the vernacular has enabled cultures around the world to bring their own particular nuances to the language of worship, while exposing new power struggles and attempts at control within the hierarchy. Nowhere are these more conspicuous than over the use of inclusive language, with Vatican officials sometimes overriding local bishops, such as those of England and Wales, in vetoing translations of liturgical texts that use inclusive language. An instruction issued by the Vatican in March 2001, *Liturgiam authenticam*, insists on the need to retain traditional uses of gender-specific language in the liturgy and forbids the use of inclusive language.[7]

However, in many situations inclusive language more faithfully reflects the traditions of the Christian faith and the languages in which it originated than the more exclusive terminology of languages such as English, which have no commonly accepted neuter term to refer to human beings of either gender. The Latin words '*homo*', '*vir*' and '*femina*' refer to respectively the human, man and woman, and it does not violate the meaning of these words to translate them in that way. In Greek, the corresponding words are '*anthropos*', '*aner*' and '*gynae*'. The language of gender was fluid in the Early and medieval Church, not only in referring to humankind but also in referring to God. To call God and Christ mother and to use the symbolism of the maternal body when referring to the deity was part of the language of Christian devotion for people such as St Ambrose, Julian of Norwich and

St Anselm. In Hebrew, the word associated with God's spirit, *ruach*, is feminine, and in the early Syriac Church the Holy Spirit was often referred to in feminine metaphors. Wisdom is always personified as a woman in the Bible, and the biblical words for wisdom (Greek '*Sophia*' and Hebrew '*Hokmah*') are feminine. In the writings of Hildegard of Bingen, all God's attributes such as wisdom, love and mercy are feminine. So when the prelates in the Vatican rule out the use of inclusive language, they are being subservient not to the dynamic and creative Spirit of God, who has manifested herself in so many forms to the human spirit, but to the suffocating spirit of a patriarchal ideology which still has them in its grip.

But they are perhaps also motivated by a concern to preserve the poetic beauty of liturgical language, both from the effects of political correctness and from the effects of 'dumbing down', which reduces the mystical power of Catholic worship to the lowest common denominator of language. Melvyn Matthews, in his book, *Both Alike to Thee*, makes an eloquent appeal for the Church to rediscover the poetic beauty of mystical language in the liturgy. He argues that in reducing liturgical language to the prosaic and mundane, we have closed off its capacity to communicate the transcendence and mystery of God: 'We make ourselves deaf with the sound of our own words and so fail to hear the original mystical speech of God who is too real, too frightening for us to face.'[8]

If the Mass is to be a gateway into the mystery of the incarnation, then its language needs to reach beyond the parlance and rhythms of everyday speech, and to acquire the musical cadences and silences of poetry. But it takes many centuries for liturgies to evolve in this way, as each generation both repeats and refines what went before. As the vernacular liturgies settle into their different cultures, as they become suffused with the breath and the voice of the worshipping community, they will acquire the mystical qualities they currently lack. This again means that if we are to remain open to the invitation of the future we must be patient, and we must also be willing to take risks, to get things wrong, to go back and start again if necessary, rather than imposing a reactionary and outworn set of rules designed to suffocate the song of God in the language of worship.

Joy and hope, grief and anguish

The transition from Latin to the vernacular is symbolic of a Church that has stopped defining herself over and against the world, and has started understanding herself as a prophetic and revelatory dimension of history and society, which exists not in isolation from but in solidarity with the whole human family. The opening words of the Vatican II *Pastoral Constitution on the Church in the Modern World* create a vision of what this amounts to:

> The joy and hope, the grief and anguish of the people of our time, especially of those who are poor or afflicted in any way, are the joy and hope, the grief and anguish of the followers of Christ as well. Nothing that is genuinely human fails to find an echo in their hearts. For theirs is a community composed of people who, united in Christ and guided by the Holy Spirit, press onwards towards the kingdom of the Father and are bearers of a message of salvation intended for all people. That is why Christians cherish a sense of deep solidarity with the human race and its history.[9]

Perhaps nobody anticipated the extent to which Catholics around the world would respond to this invitation, generating a revolution in Catholic life and thought that still sends shock waves through the Church. For non-Western Christians, Vatican

II was an invitation to inculturate the Church in the traditions and customs of their own societies. In Africa and Asia, vibrant forms of Catholicism emerged in the synthesis between local cultures and the Catholic tradition. For Catholic women, it was an invitation to bring the insights and visions of the women's movement into the Church, and thus feminist theology was born in the heady aftermath of the Council. Mary Daly, writing in the 1960s, produced a book entitled *The Church and the Second Sex*, in which she offered a cautious defence of post-conciliar Catholicism in response to Simone de Beauvoir's feminist milestone, *The Second Sex*.[10] Daly has since left the Church in a flourish of feminist rhetoric. For her, as for many other women, the promise of the Council was short-lived. It came to a decisive end with the publication of *Humanae Vitae* in 1968, with its condemnation of artificial methods of birth control.

Yet feminism still flourishes in the Catholic Church, as does support for women's ordination. It is part of a growing movement around the world in which the dignity, freedom and equality of all human beings is being reasserted, in resistance to political, religious and economic structures that overtly or insidiously perpetuate ideologies of inequality, servility and oppression, often in the name of the God they claim to serve. Many of today's religious liberation movements can be traced back to that other great awakening that drew its inspiration from Vatican II: liberation theology.

With the collapse of the intellectual barrier between Catholicism and secular thought, the theologians of Latin America began to look to the social sciences for a theological analysis that would enable them to challenge the structures of poverty and economic exploitation that oppressed their people. Borrowing selectively from Marxist theory, they embarked on the radical politicization of the Church's message, and Catholicism became closely allied with the revolutionary movements that fought against the dictatorial regimes of the 1970s. The Church's education programmes became geared towards 'conscientization', intended to awaken the poor to their own exploitation and to work in solidarity with them to usher in a new era of justice based on the politics of socialism.

In the words of Gustavo Gutiérrez's famous dictum, 'History is one.'[11] Gone was the belief, which can be traced back to Augustine's *City of God*, that the story of Christian salvation is played out in contrast to the story of secular politics and culture. For Gutiérrez and his colleagues, salvation history is human history, and the story of Christ is inseparable from the story of humankind in all its struggles and failures. This means that the Church betrays Christ when she promises justice only in heaven, life only after death and salvation beyond the here and now, offering religion as the 'opium of the people', in order to reconcile the poor to their suffering and make them passive in the face of their own exploitation. In liberation theology, salvation begins with the struggle for freedom in this world, and it entails a confrontation with the forces of evil represented by capitalism and the global economic system. It also entails unmasking the idolatries and deceptions of Western Christianity, in its failure to confront injustice and its collusion with the forces of Mammon. Gutiérrez writes, 'the great pastoral, and therefore theological, question is: How is it possible to tell the poor, who are forced to live in conditions that embody a denial of love, that God loves them?'[12]

Under the papacy of John Paul II, a number of highly conservative bishops have been appointed to replace the liberationists of the 1970s and 1980s, robbing liberation theology of much of its institutional support. At the same time, the collapse of communism and the burgeoning power of global capitalism have led to a loss of confidence in the potential for economic transformation, and the rhetoric of revolution has yielded to a more sombre and pessimistic approach in the writings of some liberation theologians. Commitment to the poor now sometimes requires the language of martyrdom rather than revolution, as for instance in Jon Sobrino's *Jesus the Liberator*, written in 1991 after the political murders of his colleagues at the University of El Salvador.[13]

Both liberation theology and feminist theology have undergone numerous upheavals and transformations in their short histories. They need to be understood as dynamic and constantly evolving movements, which are no longer confined to a few on the margins of the Church. Despite the opposition they face, they have given rise to a new religious consciousness, in which issues of social justice have become as important for many believers as questions of personal morality narrowly focused on issues of sexuality and reproduction. Many would argue that this is not an innovation but a return to an earlier and more holistic vision of Christian morality, which prevailed until the late Middle Ages. Patristic writings are informed by a Christian social conscience more radical than that which prevails in many churches today.

In the 2000-year history of Christianity, liberation theology and feminism are as yet in their nascent stages. Theological visions take centuries to evolve, to find acceptance, to discover their truth amidst the competing pressures and claims of culture and history. Inevitably, history will discover the limitations and the failings of our modern visions of freedom, just as today we find it so easy to look back and judge the past.

Perhaps we also need to acknowledge that history does not move forward in a continuous flow of progress and evolution. It is a faltering and erratic process, with moments of crisis and transformation, which work their way slowly and painfully through the social order. We cannot prevent change because we are afraid of its inevitable violence and disruption, and we risk being incapacitated if we refuse to act until we have scrutinized every aspect of our motives, intentions and their possible out-comes. I have a friend whose catch-phrase is, 'If a thing's worth doing, it's worth doing badly.' Sometimes, we have to take sides, to set aside our concern for clarity and certainty, and to risk getting it wrong. Living as we do in an era when humankind faces the magnitude of our capacity for destruction, as well as the wonder of our capacity for creativity, there is no neutral point of observation, no innocent ignorance.

The story of the Church begins with a frightened and perse-cuted handful of women and men confronted by the tyranny and power of the Roman empire. We should never underestimate what God's spirit can do, if we are open to her bright, empower-ing presence among us. In the words of Gerard Manley Hopkins' sonnet, 'God's Grandeur':

The world is charged with the grandeur of God.
    It will flame out, like shining from shook foil;
    It gathers to a greatness, like the ooze of oil
Crushed. Why do men then now not reck his rod?
Generations have trod, have trod, have trod;
    And all is seared with trade; bleared, smeared with toil;
    And wears man's smudge and shares man's smell: the soil
Is bare now, nor can foot feel, being shod.

And for all this, nature is never spent;
    There lives the dearest freshness deep down things;
And though the last light off the black West went
    Oh, morning, at the brown brink eastward, springs –
Because the Holy Ghost over the bent
    World broods with warm breast and with ah! bright wings.

Breaking and blessing

In repentance and hope we gather up past, present and future in the still small eye of eternity before God, but also never standing still, never able to grasp the passing moment. We cannot change the past, and even as we live the moment it is already history. The future rushes towards us and we are always unprepared, taken by surprise, called to act without being ready. Perhaps that is why the world's great religions all call us to nurture that inner space of eternal stillness and calm. In Christianity, the cultivation of virtue is a lifetime's work, a commitment to qualities of patience, moderation and harmony of living, which Thomas Aquinas says constitute the balance we need if we are to be happy. The virtuous person is one who can afford to act spontaneously, to respond without fear, because she is at peace with herself and with God. She is the person who greets the angel and the stranger with a *'fiat'*, opening her being to the life that calls to her from everywhere and everything, from nowhere and nothing, always providing a body of warmth for the God who comes in the guise of the unexpected and the uninvited.

In the Mass, we are called to the dying and the rising of all that is. The sacrifice of the Mass is not an offering of a victim to appease God. It is not a cultic ritual by a sacrificial priest. It is a journey into the wounded heart of the world, Christ's heart and the heart of every individual who comes with unhealed memories and unfulfilled hopes, with secret yearnings and lonely resentments, with prayers of longing and cries of abandonment. All these we bring tucked away behind our Sunday smiles, and the Spirit of God comes down upon us, and our broken dreams become our offerings, the gift of our muddled selves to God, our hunger satisfied and our thirst slaked with the bread of life and the cup of our salvation.

But Christ is not only the wounded victim of love. Christ is also the vulnerable infant of love, the lovechild of God and Mary, of creator and creation, and the Eucharist is an act of birth before and beyond the death of Christ. Christ is consecrated among us, no longer as Mary's child, but as the earth's gift of life. He is the ploughed field and the harvest, the vineyard and the fruit, the garden of creation transformed into love's food by God's grace and human work. So we bring to the Eucharist not only the wounds and the betrayals of life, we bring also the newborn promises and hopes, the fledgling visions and dreams, which need to be tended and nourished in order to flourish.

> Blessed are you, Lord, God of all creation.
> Through your goodness we have this bread to offer, which
>   earth has given and human hands have made.
> It will become for us the bread of life.

> Blessed are you, Lord, God of all creation.
> Through your goodness we have this wine to offer,
> fruit of the vine and work of human hands.
> It will become our spiritual drink.

The ancient Jewish prayer of blessing weaves together nature and culture, humanity and God, and catches everything up in a great transcendent act of healing and renewal. This is time out of time, a fragment of eternity that slips unnoticed into our everyday world. It is a time for gathering in and letting go, for harvesting and sowing, for penitence, forgiveness and hope. Here, our spirits stutter between words that can never express the enormity of our longing for wholeness and peace. Like Michelangelo's Adam, we stretch out our fingertips across the infinitely small, infinitely vast, gap which is between ourselves and God. We stand shoulder to shoulder with a multitude of strangers, and our voices are a babel that cannot build a tower to heaven. But beyond comprehension or imagination, we, the priests of creation, call down the Spirit of God upon our meagre offerings, and we dare to believe that she hears, responds and comes to live among us.

The Mass reminds us that life is a constant process of death and renewal. Repentance and forgiveness mean dying to our old attachments, habits and weaknesses, and allowing fragile but hopeful beginnings to be reborn within us. The death of Christ is the prelude to a cosmic act of rebirth, when the resurrection gathers up the whole of creation and rebirths it anew on the far side of death.

What then do death and resurrection mean for Christians today? What might we learn from the past as we search for symbols of renewal and hope for the modern world? As the Mass subsides into stillness and the crowds disperse, we travel to the outskirts of the city to Domitilla's Catacombs, to reflect on the meaning of death.

Notes

1. Catherine of Siena, *Dialogue*, p. 35.
2. See Chapter 1.
3. Mary Midgeley, *Wickedness: A Philosophical Essay* (London and New York: Ark Paperbacks, 1986), p. 199.
4. John Paul II, *Crossing the Threshold of Hope*, ed. Vittorio Messori, trans. Jenny and Martha McPhee (London: Jonathan Cape, 1994), p. 62.
5. John Paul II, *Mulieris Dignitatem: apostolic letter on the dignity and vocation of women on the occasion of the Marian year* (London: Catholic Truth Society, 1988), p. 44.
6. See John Paul II, *Evangelium Vitae: encyclical letter on the value and inviolability of human life* (London: Catholic Truth Society, 1995).
7. See *http://www.vatican.va/roman_curia/congregations/ccdds/documents/*.
8. Melvyn Matthews, *Both Alike to Thee: The Retrieval of the Mystical Way* (London: SPCK, 2000), pp. 52–3.
9. '*Gaudium et Spes*: Pastoral Constitution on the Church in the Modern

World, 7 December 1965', in Flannery, OP (ed.), *Vatican Council II*: pp. 903–1001.

10. Mary Daly, *The Church and the Second Sex* (Boston, MA: Beacon Press, 1985). See also Simone de Beauvoir, *The Second Sex*, trans. H. M. Parshley (London: Penguin, 1972).

11. See Gustavo Gutiérrez, *A Theology of Liberation: History, Politics, and Salvation* (London: SCM Press, 1988), pp. 86ff.

12. Ibid., p. xxxiv.

13. See Sobrino, *Jesus the Liberator*.

Veneranda and St Petronilla, fresco, Domitilla Catacombs

7

Death's Friendship:
Domitilla Catacombs

The jigsaw of death

I arrive at the Domitilla Catacombs early one morning, before the tour buses. These particular catacombs are in the care of the German Brothers of Mercy, and their lovingly tended gardens exude that aura of timeless serenity and gentle welcome which is so often associated with ancient graveyards. The neatly ordered flowerbeds, fountains and picnic areas, palm trees arching against a blue Roman sky, do not protest against the anarchy and disintegration of death but sanctify it with a mysterious grace.

I stand waiting for my guide in a cool antechamber, looking at a statue of Christ, the Good Shepherd. Then the first of the buses arrives, and a noisy gaggle of Japanese tourists engulfs me. 'Who is she?' asks a woman coming to stand beside me. 'It's a statue of Christ the Good Shepherd,' I reply. 'Ah, she is Jesus Christ!', and the woman proceeds to light a candle. (When in Rome...)

That little androgynous Christ, a shepherd boy with a lamb over his shoulders symbolizing the soul of the deceased, speaks of the trust and faith of the Early Church. The statue is modelled on a third-century fresco in the catacombs, so it is a very early image. It reflects the spiritual imagination of an era when Christians still identified themselves with the marginalized and poor of imperial Rome, before Christianity itself became a religion modelled on the images of kings and emperors. And that was also before the divisions of gender became firmly institutionalized in the Church, so that Christ perhaps did not bear the burden of essential masculinity with which he is invested today.

The image belongs to a time when the early Christians destabilized the structures and disrupted the boundaries of Roman society, not least in their attitudes towards the dead. Peter Brown, whose scholarship has done much to shed light on early Christian attitudes and practices, argues that it was in the relationship between the living and the dead, particularly in the cult of the saints, that Christians posed the greatest threat to the Roman world, because this undermined one of the fundamental distinctions on which so many other social distinctions rested. Brown points out that 'the rise of Christianity in the pagan world was met by deep religious anger',[1] often directed at the cult of the saints. He goes on to argue that 'the rise of the cult of saints was sensed by contemporaries, in no uncertain manner, to have broken most of the imaginative boundaries which ancient men had placed between heaven and earth, the divine and the human, the living and the dead, the town and its antithesis'.[2] So to visit the Christian catacombs is to visit those early spaces where the religious defences of the Roman empire began to crumble, not under the assault of a violent and revolutionary minority, but under the pervasive influence of a community seeking 'new forms of reverence ... with new forms of the exercise of power, new bonds of human dependence, new, intimate, hopes for protection and justice in a changing world'.[3]

It is human nature to pretend that we can cheat death through some form of posterity. For some cultures, that posterity lies in producing children. For others, it lies in enshrining one's memory in tablets of stone and human edifices, if one is wealthy enough to do so. In our media-driven postmodern culture, it lies in the desperation for what Andy Warhol called 'fifteen minutes of fame', so that there is little some people will not do to appear on television or sell their story to the tabloid press. In the ephemeral world of telecommunications and disintegrating communities, it becomes more and more difficult to believe that one's life is of enduring significance and value. Better to have appeared on 'Jerry Springer' or 'Big Brother' than never to have appeared at all.

The ancient Romans also sought to leave their mark on the future, and their pagan tombs lie side by side with those of the early Christians in the catacombs. Sometimes it is difficult to tell the two apart, since Christians did not always destroy the traces of the past when they took over such places. Seen from this great distance in time, the artefacts of death are a jigsaw with many missing pieces. As with so many other early Christian sites, the catacombs are a space of transition, not only between the living and the dead, but between two great historical movements – that of the cults of imperial Rome and that of the Christian Church. As well as the pagan and Christian burial sites, there are also the Mithraic catacombs, remains of the cult of Mithraism which flourished in the first three centuries of the Christian era.[4]

Baptizing the darkness

Mithraism originated in Persia, and its founding myth was focused on the Indian and Persian god Mithras, who slaughtered a bull, from whose dying body sprang all the earth's produce and from whose seed sprang every useful animal species. There are many apparent similarities between Mithraism and early Christianity. Both of them had strong ritualistic elements with themes of cleansing and redemption, and both celebrated *agape* feasts in honour of their gods. However, Christianity from the beginning believed that it had a universal message, which was open to all and which therefore precluded any form of esotericism or elitism.

Its rite of initiation was baptism, preceded by a time of preparation in the faith as a catechumen. The early Christians also believed that the shedding of Christ's blood was the ultimate sacrifice, symbolically re-enacted in the bloodless sacrifice of the Eucharist. Mithraism was an exclusive and esoteric male cult with several levels of initiation, the culmination of which was a ritual involving the sacrifice of a bull to Mithras and an initiation ceremony that involved immersion in its blood. This was known as the ritual of the *Magna Mater*, during which, participants believed, the steaming blood of the bull cleansed them of all impurities.

The universality of their message and the non-violence of their rituals set the early Christians apart from their pagan neighbours. If today, even in a post-Christian society, we experience a sense of horror over practices such as the cult of Mithras, this perhaps affirms Girard's suggestion that Christianity has over the centuries effected a fundamental transformation in Western attitudes to violence.[5] Although this has failed to curb the militarism and oppressive power of Christian nations, it has seeped through Western consciousness at many other levels. Sacrifice and bloodshed are not religious aberrations but are the normal ways in which human beings have always worshipped their gods. Girard suggests that the cross of Christ is the ultimate protest against this understanding of a god who demands violence, for on the cross God becomes the victim of the sacrifice and therefore exposes its true motivation in the scapegoating violence of the crowd (See chapter 2).

So, with our imaginations overlaid by centuries of Christian conditioning, it is difficult for modern minds to read about cults such as Mithraism without some sense of revulsion, but Girard would argue that we are far more vulnerable to these orientations to violence than we acknowledge. At the time of writing, the execution of Timothy McVeigh has just been publicly witnessed by journalists and relatives of his victims, suggesting the extent to which primitive bloodlust lurks very close to the surface of our modern societies. If technology provides for bloodless and sanitized forms of killing, it does nothing to address the ancient instincts that drive human beings to a murderous desire for vengeance, which insists on meeting violence with violence.

Some modern pagans reject Christianity in favour of religious beliefs that can accommodate darkness as well as light, violence as well as peace, arguing that Christianity has had a repressive effect on human consciousness and society. Some appeal for the unleashing of the forces of the unconscious as a powerful spiritual resource, and often, although not always, this goes hand in hand with a quest for a revitalized masculine religious identity.[6] I have already argued that Christianity has yet to accommodate paganism, and until it does it will always be burdened with a dark and unexamined dimension of fear closely associated with Eve, sexuality and death. The rehabilitation of Eve entails making peace with death, and accepting the sense of mortality that the Book of Genesis attributes to her in the formation of consciousness and the acquisition of knowledge.

But in facing the darkness Christians must also baptize it. There is a difference between letting loose the violence of unbaptized desire – a violence that pervades Western attitudes to sexuality – and liberating ourselves individually and collectively to enjoy the happiness of lives harmoniously balanced by moderation, gentleness and self-control. This difference might be symbolically represented by the Mithraic and Christian catacombs, with their echoes through the centuries of two simultaneous cults, both of which had widespread appeal, one founded on secrecy and violence and the other on openness and peace. In the underground caverns of the human unconscious, these are still the alternatives that seduce, invite and compel us.

Death's enigma

Although one can approach the catacombs with a keen sense of historical enquiry, they also speak of the unavoidability and enigma of death. What is one to make of these human bones and artefacts, all that remains of a persecuted community that dared to proclaim its faith in the resurrection of the body to a disbelieving and hostile world? Are these naked skeletons signs that mock the hubristic fantasy of redemption, or are they an invitation into some promise beyond the visible, tangible world we know, into a realm of bodily transformation and wholeness?

The guide takes me down passages normally closed to visitors, encouraged by my interest in theology, so that we can escape the tourists. I follow him down rough, narrow corridors, with the tombs of men, women and children rising on either side. The walls are almost soft to the touch, carved out of the volcanic stone, tufa, on which Rome is built. He shows me a skeleton, remarkably preserved, a *memento mori* more real and awe-inspiring than the carved effigies and skulls in some of Rome's churches. Who was that person, and what would she have said to a Christian woman at the beginning of the third millennium? What slender threads of humanity and hope still link my life to hers, allowing perhaps for promises of heaven to pass from generation to generation until maybe, one day, our voices will sing together in the presence of God?

Such musings are not fashionable among some modern theologians. Rosemary Radford Ruether argues that it is a sign of egotism to want to live forever. She writes that

> the problem of personal immortality is created by an effort to absolutize personal or individual ego as itself everlasting, over against the total community of being. To the extent to which we have transcended egoism for relation to community,

we can also accept death as the final relinquishment of individuated ego into the great matrix of being.[7]

Ruether's caution is appropriate in an individualistic society in which the ego is set over against the community, but I am unconvinced that such an opposition is universally valid. There are many shades of individuated existence between the solitary Western ego and absorption into the oneness of being. The catacombs evoke both the individuality of the human being, who is mourned and remembered by his and her loved ones and entrusted to the care of God, and the community of the Early Church, which shared a collective vision of the redemption and restoration of the cosmos.

In a searing attack on the doctrine of the Assumption, Mary Daly refers to the 'nonbiodegradable assumed virgin',[8] but in the catacombs we are left in no doubt about the biodegradability of the body, Christian or otherwise. Faced with this silent witness, contemplating the disintegration of the body to bones and dust, belief in the resurrection involves a leap of faith that is perhaps impossible for many modern Christians.

But these ancient Christian burial sites do not suggest arrogance and hubris in the face of death. They are holy ground, sanctified by the quiet presence of hope amidst the disintegration of death. These were democratic burial sites, where those excluded from the lavish burial rites of wealthy Romans decomposed side by side with the Christian aristocracy. And death in such a place was not a romantic form of escapism, such as it risks becoming to modern visitors who breathe in the damp, earthy smell of bodies long returned to dust and nature. The catacombs were foetid places of decomposing bodies whose smell could not be masked by all the fragrant oils and herbs of anointing. If we moderns think that reason should make us sceptical about the resurrection of the body, how much more sceptical should those early Christians have been in that world of early and violent death and often anonymous burial?

Nor was the grief and terror of death diminished by its promise. The tombs of children are a poignant reminder that widespread infant mortality does not diminish the parents' sense of loss. There is four-year-old Christa, whose family dog appears on her tombstone, and a four-month-old baby in the hollow above her. Describing the horror felt by Gregory of Nyssa when contemplating the dead body of his sister Macrina, Brown writes that 'The "shining way to Paradise" of Christian art and liturgy had in no way rendered translucent the facts of death for the average Mediterranean man.'[9]

But for all the material potency of death's presence, Domitilla's Catacombs are a place of beauty, as if the trusting vision of their silent occupants has indeed transcended the limits of their mortal lives. It is a place that invites belief, perhaps because in the universal solidarity of death, hope too finds a sense of solidarity and communion beyond the grave. That is the basis on which the cult of the saints was founded. Our own salvation is precarious, fraught with possibilities of failure and rejection. God is just as well as merciful, and, judging ourselves too harshly, we dread that justice will in the end triumph and we will get what we think we deserve. The catacombs grew up around the tombs of martyrs, because however weak one's own commitment, these were people who had 'fought the good fight' and were sure to be with Christ in heaven. But they were also friends of the living, and an abundance of grace and good works could be shared among those of more frugal accomplishments.

The cult of the saints

Protestantism has never really understood the psychological and social value of the cult of the saints. Founded upon an isolated individualism in its theology of redemption, it does not see that in the community of the redeemed everything is held in common, even virtue and goodness. The incarnate Christ, saviour of the world, is born into a community of redeeming love because he is born of a woman whose 'yes' is the first salvific response to God. His saving work is continued after his death in the community of the Church, when we stand not alone but as a collective body, which is both redeemed and redeemer. This has led to pernicious theological claims of exclusivity over the centuries, in the doctrine of *extra ecclesia, nulla salus* – outside the church there is no salvation – but it also serves as a reminder that being is a state of being in relationship, and no one, not even or especially not God, is ever alone. We are neither created nor redeemed alone. God is three persons, co-dependent, never acting in isolation but always in the form of a love among persons, which evokes, invites, calls, responds. The Church is part of that eternal invocation and response of love, and it means that the Christian has privileged access to the insight that personhood, love and communion are inseparable even in God. Thus the autonomous individual, cut off from others, is also in some sense cut off from the image of God. Perhaps that is why the Western ideology of the subject developed in the aftermath of the Enlightenment, with its substitution of philosophical theism for the trinitarian faith of the Church.

The Church's doctrine of salvation can be interpreted as one not of exclusivity but of inclusivity. One cannot be saved alone, any more than one can save oneself. Indeed, surely there would be no worse hell than a solitary redemption – an eternity lived out of relationship, in lonely perfection. So the cult of the saints is not a distraction from or a substitute for the uniquely redemptive love of Christ, but an affirmation of its cosmic power. Nothing, not even death, can separate us from that love, and if we are in the love of Christ then we are of necessity still in the love of the living, for Christ is supreme among the living. We are the poor neighbours of the saints in heaven, and their sainthood is nothing more or less than the eternal continuation of their love of God expressed through love of neighbour.

The cult of the saints is also an alternative version of history, one that escapes the charge that history is always written by the victors. Of course, there are militant and triumphal popes amongst the saints, though we should remember that Dante consigned some popes to hell. But most of the saints are ordinary human beings, their lives transformed not by power or wealth but by the vitalizing passion of faith, and many of them were the victims of the institutional Church. Not only that, but the cult of the saints transcends hierarchies of gender as well as of race and class, so that it is a vast population that constitutes a truly representative history of faith, hope and love. One of the most famous wall-paintings in the catacombs of Domitilla is that showing the Roman lady Veneranda being led into Paradise by her patron, St Petronilla. Like the later mosaics of the Nativity of the Virgin, it is a reminder that solidarity between women had symbolic significance in the premodern Church and accorded the female body a space of community and friendship amidst the redeemed. The patron was a person one went to for teaching and instruction, so the relationship between Veneranda and Petronilla suggests one in which Christian women turned to one another for education. Elizabeth Stuart proposes that the image of friendship might be more appropriate than patronage from a feminist point of view, and that through the reclamation of the friendship of the saints, it might be possible to develop a feminist theology of sainthood. She argues that

> Feminism has for a long time drawn attention to the radical
> individualism that permeates capitalism and Protestantism,
> giving human beings the impression that they are on their

own, in competition with others and that they need to struggle against others to survive. The relationship of women to their saints demonstrates that they are not 'on their own' but part of a common struggle that stretches back into the night of the past and forward into the morning mist of the future.[10]

Of course, this is not to deny that the men of the Church have had power over the process of canonization, and Stuart does not overlook the considerable difficulties involved in the creation of a feminist cult of the saints. But it is also important to recognize that the process of beatification and canonization has tended to follow rather than initiate popular devotion, and indeed it is debatable whether the hierarchy could ever successfully manipulate a saint into a position of widespread popularity. The most beloved and popular saints are local heroes and heroines, people who usually symbolize something culturally specific as well as universally true of the Christian faith. The saints continue the work of the incarnation by embodying Christ in every culture and class, in women and men. They remind us that between the living and the dead, what appears to the living as an unbridgeable chasm is a porous membrane through which the entreaties, prayers and hopes of ordinary human beings can permeate and sometimes, if we know how to listen, find an answering voice.

It was the desire to be close to the saints that led to Christian burial sites being situated around the tombs of martyrs. The catacombs of Domitilla grew up around the tombs of the martyrs Nereus and Achilleus, who were victims of the persecutions unleashed by the emperors Decius and Valerian in AD 250 and 257 and by Diocletian in AD 303. Flavia Domitilla was a noble woman, granddaughter of the emperor Vespasian and niece of Domitian. Her husband, Flavio Clemente, was a consul who was condemned to death by Domitian in AD 95, and Domitilla was exiled to the island of Ventotene. They were charged with 'atheism', a frequent charge against the early Christians because of their refusal to believe in the Roman gods or participate in their religious rituals. These catacombs therefore function on many levels as a symbol of inspiration for modern women: they remind us not only of the patronage of influential women such as Domitilla in the Early Church but also of their courage and perseverance in the face of persecution.

The cult of the saints can help us to reconcile our desire for personal continuity beyond the grave with our need to accept the finitude and transience of our individual egos. Stuart suggests that we might draw on a panentheistic image of the earth as the body of God, to accept that our selves are 'Taken into God [where] they become compost, nourishing future generations, aiding them to flourish if they use the legacy wisely.'[11] She goes on to argue that such a vision does not preclude the possibility of evoking individual saints through imagination and play, endowing them with the characteristics of friendship that sustain and nurture us in our own lives of faith.

The anonymity of death

But when we pause to consider the reality of death at the beginning of the third millennium, another question arises. Today the world seems more divided than ever before between the dying of the privileged and individuated few and the dying of the anonymous masses of humankind. Beyond the elaborate funerals of the wealthy, the media confront us with images of death on a scale that mocks the very notion of the uniqueness of the individual human being. We might contrast the way in which the death of Diana, Princess of Wales, captured the imagination of the world, while so many others, equal in their humanity, die without ceremony or mourning. Today we count the neglected and slaughtered dead in unnamed millions. The United Nations estimates that half a million children die each year as a result of the debt crisis, and AIDS is ravaging the peoples of Africa in numbers too horrifying to contemplate. Our television screens show images of human suffering we cannot comprehend, and behind all these lurks the unthinkable possibility of nuclear or environmental annihilation. Death in ancient catacombs or in tranquil cemeteries might masquerade as a benevolent transition between states of being, but death also confronts us in the form of the skeletons of Cambodia and Rwanda, the piles of human hair and teeth at Auschwitz, the emaciated corpses of the victims of famine.

The early Christians celebrated Christ's triumph over death, but they also regarded death rather than sin as the great enemy of humankind. Our sinfulness was not a condition of evil but of vulnerability. Satan, holding the power of death, had deceived Adam and Eve and enslaved them, and they were helpless in the grip of death. It was only when death pitted its power against God incarnate in Christ that it was overcome and humankind was liberated.[12] In celebrating this cosmic act of liberation, the early Christians were also acknowledging the awesome power and tyranny of death. It was the enormity of the enemy they faced that made the victory of Christ so significant.

Today, reason and secularism have purged Western society of the language of sin and the devil, and such words now belong only within the rantings of those deemed religious fanatics. But if these words are archaic, the feelings they describe are still real. We still experience the power of death as some alien presence, an unwanted intruder that seizes us unawares and generates overwhelming feelings of guilt, failure and terror. Lacking the language of forgiveness, redemption and liberation from death's power, we have once again become death's slaves, captive both to its terror and its fascination. We surround our children with cordons of fear, depriving them of the most basic freedoms of childhood because we refuse to accept the truth of their mortality. We demand increasingly costly and unethical means of creating, preserving and destroying life, so that in our frantic attempts to master death we become ever more distracted and obsessed by it. Thus death becomes the master of our world, depriving us of the gift of freedom that the early Christians recognized as the most precious gift of Christ to humankind.

Our avoidance of the inevitability of death finds its counterpoint in a culture that has a morbid fascination with death as glamorized fiction. We run away from the face of death as a natural fact of life and transform it instead into the ultimate cultural artefact – the dead body as Hollywood entertainment in the form of the beautiful victim of rape or the gourmet meal for a cannibalistic killer. Some writers use the term 'necrophilia' to describe this cultural malaise, which is summed up in an Easter editorial in the *Guardian* newspaper. It claims that

> the torture and brutal death of a gentle Galilean carpenter … challenges two of our most powerful contemporary taboos, death and suffering. In a competitive, capitalist culture, success is the preoccupation and happiness is the great dream. Death and suffering have no place in either. We are fascinated by death, but only death that has been glamorised or turned into whodunnit drama. Meanwhile we tidy away the reality of everyday death into crematoria and hospitals. Equally, our culture sees little meaning or purpose in suffering when Easter is above all else a celebration of the redemptive power of suffering.[13]

Befriending death

All the world's great religious traditions and philosophies acknowledge that there is a creative aspect to suffering, and they also teach us how to live creatively in the face of death. Medieval Christians used to prepare themselves for 'a good death', one in which the soul takes its leave of this world in a state of forgiveness and grace. A Christian friend recently told me how, as her aged mother lay peacefully dying, the children and grandchildren gathered around the bed to wave her goodbye and sing her on her way, promising that they would see her again in heaven. Perhaps that is not everybody's idea of an ideal send-off, but it speaks of a different attitude towards death from that which we so often encounter in our world today. In the midst of writing this today, I had a telephone call to say that a dear friend who has been suffering from cancer had died peacefully in her home, with one of her sons at her bedside. She is a Christian who has suffered a great deal in life, but she made peace with her approaching death and said her farewells with a resignation that was not lacking in joy. In our culture's collective rebellion against religion, we also experience a collective rejection of the spiritual and ethical resources, accumulated over countless generations, that might help us to cope with the unchanging challenges of death and mortality.

The illusion that life must be happy, carefree and pain-free means that, in its most vulnerable and dependent states, life becomes more and more a nuisance or a commodity, less and less the *locus* of an absolute and inviolable sanctity. The way we discuss these issues in terms of euthanasia, abortion, research on embryos and the disposability of life, suggests that we have reached a decisive moment in Western attitudes towards the meaning of life.

For two thousand years Christianity has inculcated in Western consciousness the idea of the intrinsic value of human life. This has not prevented the widespread destruction of life by Christians, but it has created a common ethos in which humanity rather than cultural, religious or ethnic identity is the hallmark of personhood, and in which the most dependent members of society have a claim upon the rich and the powerful. Indeed, one could ask how much Western medical science has been driven by the Christian imperative to alleviate suffering and to encompass every human being within the ambit of its compassion and care. In post-Christian society we are rapidly reverting to a situation in which human life has relative rather than absolute value, as a result of which the Catholic Church is insisting on an ever more absolutist position. To stand before the quiet face of death in the catacombs is to question both these approaches.

Certainly, the early Christians disrupted pagan values in their concern for the newborn, the weak and the socially vulnerable. But this concern for the life of others was matched by a sometimes cavalier willingness to become martyrs themselves. Indeed, some patristic writers lament the enthusiasm with which their contemporaries were willing to contemplate grizzly and brutal deaths at the hands of their Roman persecutors. Ever since, there has been in some aspects of Christian spirituality an unhealthy tendency towards masochism, from the hair-shirts and instruments of torture worn by some ascetics to the vigorous denial of the body's natural appetites and desires. Christians need to acquire a sense of proportion about the body from conception to death, and to learn to celebrate the body's natural desires and pleasures within the harmonious moderation of the virtuous life. This might mean defending the right to die as well as the right to life.[14] As science becomes ever more strenuous in its efforts to master life and death, there is an increasing tendency to prolong life artificially beyond any hope of recovery or healing. *Evangelium Vitae* refers to the right to forego 'aggressive medical treatment ... when death is clearly imminent and inevitable.'[15] Too often, a so-called pro-life stance becomes an obsessive preoccupation with preserving life at all costs, when Christian love might entail recognizing a terminally ill person's right to die with dignity and peace.

Religion teaches us how to befriend death, and perhaps that is why secularism is often dominated by the fear of death. In Buddhism one is encouraged to meditate deeply on the circumstances of one's own death and the processes of bodily disintegration. This is an exercise that appears morbid to the modern, sanitized mind, but it is intended to serve as a reminder of the transience and finitude of all things and therefore as a path to the peace of non-attachment. In Christianity, the cross has always been the supreme focus for imaginative encounters with death. In the reflections of Julian of Norwich, the fourteenth-century English mystic, she graphically describes the physical changes in the dying Christ:

> I saw His sweet face as if it were dry and bloodless, pale with dying. Next it became more pale and dead-looking with increasing weakness, and then it turned more dead-looking, to blue and then to brown-blue as the flesh continued more and more to die.... This deep dying caused a change pitiful to watch. The nose clogged and dried as I watched, and the sweet body was brown and black, changed entirely from His own fair, life-like color to dry dying.

This reflection continues for several pages, drawing her more and more deeply into the reality of Christ's suffering until she reaches a cathartic moment of liberation and joy:

> And just at the moment that it seemed to me that life could last no longer, and the showing of the end must, of necessity, be near, suddenly, looking at the same cross, I saw Him transform His blessed face. The transformation of His blessed face transformed mine, and I was as glad and merry as it was possible to be.[16]

This capacity to meditate on the effects of death as a means to coming to the joy of life is not the exclusive prerogative of the religious imagination. Jim Crace's novel, *Being Dead*, is a moving meditation on the processes of death and decay, which in its avowedly materialist approach allows the body no glimmer of transcendence or personal resurrection.[17] Yet it is an exquisitely crafted love-story which explores in the most poetic and disturbing imagery the life-giving realities of bodily decomposition. It is a book about two married, middle-aged academics whose murdered bodies lie side by side on a beach and, before their discovery, become host to many different forms of life even as they gradually subside into formlessness and disintegration. It is not a religious book, but it is a profound protest against our cultural insensitivity to the mysterious transformations of death. Ultimately, it hints at a joyful celebration of the capacity of life to renew continually and nurture itself on death.

The catacombs are not an easy encounter with death. They are in many ways much closer to Crace's vision of a thoroughly material world of decomposition and natural life processes than to any Christian vision of the resurrection. In the end, only hope separates the believer from the non-believer in this place of death. The Christian looks at the dust and bone of the catacombs and deciphers in them the strange hieroglyphics of the hope of redemption. The atheist might decipher them as the pathetic illusion of faith, the ultimate evidence of the folly of belief.

We need no evidence of death, for it is all around us. But when we speak of resurrection, we must come up out of the earth where culture is silenced by nature's power, and venture again into the realm of creativity, art and imagination. We cannot encounter the resurrection. Nobody witnesses the moment when Christ rises from the grave, and even his closest disciples do not recognize him at first. This suggests that whatever it means to speak of rising from the dead, it is a realm of the most profound and impenetrable mystery. But the image of the resurrection, however enigmatic, finds rich and varied expression in Christian art. So to contemplate what it means to believe in the resurrection of the dead, we need to return to the land of the living and reflect upon the ways in which to be human is to express an eternity of hope, which refuses to let death have the last word.

Notes

1. Peter Brown, *The Cult of the Saints: Its Rise and Function in Latin Christianity* (Chicago, IL: The University of Chicago Press, 1981), p. 6.
2. Ibid., p. 21.
3. Ibid., p. 22.
4. See Ivana della Portella, *Subterranean Rome*, photos Mark E. Smith (Rome: Konemann, 1999), pp. 15–55.
5. See Chapter 2.
6. See the discussion in Dave Green, 'From Tree to Rhizome: Pagan Spirituality, Science and Resistance in the New Millenium', in Ursula King (ed.), *Spirituality and Society in the New Millennium* (Brighton: Sussex Academic Press, 2001): pp. 206–19.
7. Rosemary Radford Ruether, *Sexism & God-Talk* (London: SCM Press, 1992), p. 257–8.
8. Mary Daly, *Pure Lust: Elemental Feminist Philosophy* (London: The Women's Press, 1984), p. 127.
9. Brown, *The Cult of the Saints*, p. 70.
10. Elizabeth Stuart, *Spitting at Dragons: Towards a Feminist Theology of Sainthood* (London: Mowbrays, 1996), p. 92.
11. Ibid., p. 115.
12. See G. Aulén, *Christus Victor: An Historical Study of the Three Main Types of the Idea of the Atonement*, trans. A. G. Hebert (London: SPCK, 1961).
13. *Guardian*, 14 April 2001, p. 21.
14. See Hans Jonas, Ph.D., 'The Right to Die' in Thomas A. Shannon (ed.), *Bioethics*, 3rd edn (Mahwah, NJ: St Pauls, 1997): pp. 195–208.
15. *Evangelium Vitae*, n. 65, p. 117.
16. Julian of Norwich, *The Revelation of Divine Love*, trans. M.-L. del Mastro (Tunbridge Wells: Burns & Oates, 1994), p. 94.
17. See Jim Crace, *Being Dead* (London: Penguin, 2000).

The Resurrection, Pericle Fazzini, Paul VI Concert Hall

8

Love's Resurrection:
The Paul VI Concert Hall

The dancing Christ and the dancing women

A large icon of the annunciation is carried in procession down
the aisle of the Paul VI concert hall, adjacent to St Peter's. The
procession is led by Indian women in brightly coloured saris,
carrying baskets of rose petals and burning incense. They mount
the marble steps to the stage, with Pericle Fazzini's vast bronze
sculpture of the resurrection swirling above them.

This was the opening of a jubilee concert in honour of Mary,
directed and performed mainly by women from all over the
world. The evening began with an Iranian Muslim women's
ensemble singing verses from the Qur'ān, and for the next two
hours we were swept up in a celebration of music and dance that
seemed to emanate from a different universe to the baroque
extravagance of the basilica next door. Here, the extravagance lay
not in the brash proclamation of Rome's power frozen in marble
and bronze but in the human body and voice – the female body
and voice – transformed into a living icon of praise. Peruvian
dancers, American sopranos, a Filipino choir, African, Polish and
Romanian musicians, Korean women like bright butterflies in
their national dress – that night the Vatican was truly catholic,
and woman was truly incarnate. The evening ended with a group
of young Italian ballet dancers, dressed in slinky costumes in the

colours of the jubilee logo. As they writhed sinuously up the steps and arched their backs and raised their arms to the risen Christ, I wanted to pinch myself. Could this possibly be happening on the Pope's doorstep? This was Eve risen, redeemed, beautiful, sexy, dancing where she should always have danced, in the heart of Christ's Church on earth.

Fazzini's sculpture was a perfect backdrop to the occasion. It shows Christ rising out of a hell of abstract, tormented shapes with tatters of flesh and human bone almost recognizable amidst the chaos of death. Bare branches claw up towards the sky, evoking countless battlefields and scenes of nuclear desolation. In the midst of it all, the body of Christ takes shape. Like Bernini's Daphne, his lower limbs are in a state of mutation, still lost amidst the entanglement of decay. But as the gaze is drawn up along his shimmering torso to his raised arms and windswept hair, a sense of exhilaration takes hold. If Bernini's Daphne is forever trapped in a moment of metamorphosis symbolizing the loss of her humanity, Fazzini's Christ stands poised forever in the moment of metamorphosis when humanity rises from the grave to eternity. His head is tilted and his arms raised as if he is summoning the cosmos to join him in the dance of creation redeemed. That night, the dancing women obeyed his summons and rose through two thousand years of silence to echo that distant *fiat*, that woman's 'yes', which all the 'noes' of history have not stifled.

Referring to the appointment of Patricia Adkins Chiti as director of the concert, the programme draws attention to the fact that 'this is the first time, in the history of the Jubilees, that a Pontifical Organization has chosen a woman for such an important undertaking, and the principal players in this evening are also women.' Later, I met Adkins Chiti. She told me of the obstructiveness of the cardinals and their apparent determination that the event should not take place. Despite the millions spent on the jubilee celebrations, in the end she had to raise money privately because the cardinal in charge of finance refused her sufficient funding. Afterwards, she heard that the Pope had expressed his pleasure that the concert had gone ahead. Such stories are a reminder that even the smallest symbolic gains for women come about through determination, struggle and resistance. The female body has yet to experience the promise of the resurrection in the body of the Church.

That is why women today might creatively lay claim to the Western Church's belief that the sexual body has ontological significance – that we are created, redeemed and resurrected as male and female in God's image. In the words of St Augustine:

> Now the sex of the female derives not from a disorder, but from nature, a nature freed henceforth from the marriage union and from child-bearing. All the same, the female organism will survive, not indeed to serve its previous function, but enhanced with a new beauty, a beauty that will not excite concupiscence, which will have disappeared, but will serve to glorify the wisdom and mercy of God, who created what before did not exist, and who has freed from corruption that which He created.[1]

However ambivalent Augustine's theological legacy, his insistence on the integrity and beauty of the female body – not as a sex object positioned by the scopophilia of the male gaze, not as a wifely chattel, not as a body defined by motherhood, but as a person created for God's delight – opens into a playground of the imagination, in which a woman might give creative shape to an eternally sanctified body. But what does it mean to say this, and can we moderns possibly agree even in the imagination to a doctrine as incredible as the resurrection of the body? Perhaps one can only circle round the idea of resurrection, exploring its possibilities, clothing in words a body that cannot be touched or held or imagined and yet can nevertheless be intimated, hoped for, and maybe even promised by God.

Nuclear transfigurations

I have already referred to objections by some theologians regarding the risk of egotism inherent in the doctrine of the resurrection of the body. Mary Daly goes further and links the doctrine of Mary's Assumption with the development of the atomic bomb. She compares images of Mary clothed in the sun with the intensity of light generated by a nuclear explosion. Both, she argues, are images that are about death and man's triumph over death. She quotes the science writer William Lawrence, who exemplifies the 'doublethink' of attitudes towards nuclear deterrence in his description of watching the first atomic explosion:

> This great iridescent cloud and its mushroom top, I found myself thinking as I watched, is actually a protective umbrella that will forever shield mankind everywhere against threat of annihilation in any atomic war. This rising supersun seemed to me the symbol of the dawn of a new era in which any sizable war had become impossible; for no aggressor could now start a war without the certainty of absolute and swift annihilation.[2]

Such beliefs were used to defend the policy of MAD (Mutually Assured Destruction), by which America believed it could forever keep at bay the 'evil empire' of Russia. Later, I want to listen to Russian women's voices in the aftermath of Chernobyl, offering a very different perspective on the experience of a nuclear explosion.

It is hard to deny that Christianity has contributed towards the creation of a dominant global culture in which the combination of imperial pride and militarism has brought the world to the brink of catastrophe. It is also difficult to know what role Christian beliefs about immortality and resurrection have played in this devaluation and exploitation of life on earth. Grace Jantzen argues persuasively that Christianity's investment in transcendence and life after death has made it a profoundly life-denying and destructive religion. In engagement with thinkers such as Irigaray, she proposes as an alternative an immanentist, pantheistic spirituality, in which maternity provides metaphors of embodiment and fruitfulness but also of mortality and vulnerability, as the basis for a new ethical and religious vision focused on this life, its injustices and its promises.[3]

The feminist perspectives offered by Ruether, Daly, Jantzen and others invite us to pause for thought and to ask ourselves what is at stake in belief in the resurrection. Is it true that we would be better off inhabiting a religious world constructed out of metaphors of the body, nature and mortality, without the nuclear brilliance of immortality? The bombing of Hiroshima on 6 August 1945 was on the Feast of the Transfiguration, when Christians celebrate Christ's transformation into the glowing presence of the divine before his disciples. 'There in their presence he was transfigured: his face shone like the sun and his clothes became as white as the light' (Matthew 17:2). For many of us, it is impossible to sit through the liturgy on that day without imagining those other ghastly transfigurations described by Japanese survivors of the atom bomb. One woman, Takeharu Terao, describes how, as a schoolgirl, she was checking the attendance register when 'a bluish white light flashed like an electric welding spark ... The world went white.'[4] A woman from Chernobyl describes her husband's fear as he lay dying of radiation sickness:

'He wrote in our notebook, "When I die, burn my body. I don't want you to be afraid." Why did he decide that? Well, you know the rumours, that Chernobyl victims "glow" even after death.'[5]

The glowing victims of Hiroshima and Chernobyl superimpose a disturbing new layer of images on Henry Vaughan's poetic vision of eternity:

> I saw Eternity the other night
> Like a great ring of pure and endless light,
>   All calm, as it was bright,
> And round beneath it, Time, in hours, days, years
>   Driven by the spheres
> Like a vast shadow moved, in which the world
>   And all her train her hurl'd.

In this age of lost innocence, Vaughan's ring of light becomes a mushroom cloud spreading over us, hurling us into a shadow world in which the hours and days and years unfold in the haunted silence of extinction. What foolish dreamer then would speak of resurrection, would risk evoking the image of the flash that instantaneously changes the very cells of life?

> I will tell you something that has been secret: that we are not all going to die, but we shall all be changed. This will be instantaneous, in the twinkling of an eye, when the last trumpet sounds. It will sound, and the dead will be raised, imperishable, and we shall be changed as well, because our present perishable nature must put on imperishability and this mortal nature must put on immortality (I Corinthians 15:51–3).

Paul had only the Romans to contend with. Perhaps it is easier to dream of resurrecting the body crucified or torn apart by lions than the body instantaneously changed, 'in the twinkling of an eye', to radioactive dust.

Imaginative resurrections

Christian speculations about the resurrection have taken the body very seriously. Medieval Christians were preoccupied with questions such as the fate of the body eaten by a cannibal, or dismembered or mutilated before death. From our position of rational modernity we might smile at such follies, but perhaps they invite us to reconsider the significance and value we attach to the human body, not because it is lifted out of and redeemed from this corrupt and condemned world, but because it belongs within the materiality of creation, which is destined for glory with God. To quote St Paul again, in a rich metaphor of maternity and birth, 'creation still retains the hope of being freed, like us, from its slavery to decadence, to enjoy the same freedom and glory as the children of God. From the beginning till now the entire creation, as we know, has been groaning in one great act of giving birth' (Romans 8:20–2).

How does our vision of the Christian story change if we begin to see it as a story about pregnancy and birth rather than about sin and death, if our suffering is not the anguish of dying but the anguish of birthing? A woman who has experienced childbirth knows that there is an extreme where the body melts into its own agony, and it matters little whether one is birthing or dying. For many mothers, birth ends in death of either the child or the mother. Is it possible to transform this into another birth, a birth into eternity? What kind of birth would this be? The newborn eternally captured at the moment of its first gasping, dying breath? The foetus aborted in the first few weeks of cellular existence? The old and weary body, which does not crave eternal life but only release and the sleep of eternity? Our medieval forebears would have understood such questions and the need to ask them. St Paul would have dismissed them contemptuously: 'Someone may ask, "How are dead people raised, and what sort of body do they have when they come back?" They are stupid questions' (I Corinthians 15:35–6).

Today, many Christians would agree, but unlike Paul they would see the stupidity of such questions as evidence that faith in bodily resurrection is a delusion. Yet it is interesting that some of those who most vehemently deny the possibility of individual, physical resurrection are feminist theologians who write eloquently about the need to overcome Christian dualism and reaffirm the goodness of the body and the earth. What greater affirmation is there than to insist on the eternal significance of creation? Christianity teaches that the material world is not an illusion but has its own dignity and purpose, which can never be destroyed. Creation will not sink back into the undifferentiated oneness from which it originated. The doctrine of the Assumption tells us that Mary's womanly body assumed into heaven is a foretaste of the redemption of all creation. The doctrine was promulgated in 1950, and some think it was in part a protest against the indiscriminate destruction of the body during the Holocaust and the Second World War. A priest friend of mine points out that, whether intentionally or not, the Catholic Church declared in 1950 that the body of a Jewish woman was the first to occupy a privileged space beside Christ in eternity.

The doctrine of the resurrection is creation's promise of infinite significance. The diversity and harmony of the created world, its music of birdsong and laughter, its feasting and loving, its trees, rivers, mountains, oceans and skies, its species and creatures, its male and female bodies, all rejoice and give thanks for the blessing of existence. The cosmos is a vast symphony of God's eternal joy in creation, and the human voice is uniquely gifted, uniquely chosen, to put words to the music and to sing creation's joy to God. And if one day we were visited by green Martians or purple Andromedans, or any of the other fantasy creatures with which we humans have peopled the universe, then that would only add to the abundance and wonder of God's creative delight. Indeed, the excesses and flights of the human imagination might themselves be imitations of the inexhaustible, childlike desire of God to go on creating, sleeping and waking, dreaming and making. Always, as God's co-creators, we are at work, making, unmaking and remaking worlds, because there is no end to it. Creation is infinite.

And in this creative history of ours we are building the city of God. The Christian story begins in a garden, but it ends in a city. The transformation of nature into culture is not a violation of God's purpose. When we human beings sculpt and carve the natural world into a great edifice of work and play, we do not violate it but call it into the future with us. So often we are drawn into a bleak and hopeless condemnation of our capacity to mould the world. Many modern thinkers depict the human, and particularly the male human, as the enemy rather than the friend of creation, so that it can be refreshing to read a polemic of praise by Camille Paglia, *enfant terrible* of American feminism:

> When I cross the George Washington Bridge or any of America's great bridges, I think: men have done this. Construction is a sublime male poetry. When I see a giant crane passing on a flatbed truck, I pause in awe and reverence, as one would for a church procession. What power of conception, what grandiosity: these cranes tie us to ancient Egypt, where monumental architecture was first imagined and achieved. If civilization had been left in female hands, we would still be living in grass huts. A contemporary woman clapping on a hard hat merely enters a conceptual system invented by men.[6]

It remains to be seen whether the participation of women will significantly change the face of culture, and it is always possible to condemn the achievements of history to date as an unrelieved story of masculine assertiveness. The architectural beauty of a Gothic church can be seen as a phallic monument to God in man's image, precursor to monstrosities such as the Trump Towers in New York where man rises proudly over the world and does not even need God to justify his erections. The city, which began as a space of human cohabitation and co-operation, is built by Cain, who already had his brother's blood on his hands. Today, the city is a human sink-pool, polluted, violent, corrupt, where faceless humanity jostles and struggles to carve out some small space of being, of individuation, amidst its obliterating anonymity. But many of us love the city, not in spite of but because of its bustling, vibrant persistence, its brash insistence that, somehow, all life is here, and maybe it is here that heaven is being built.

Against the anonymity and facelessness of death, symbolized perhaps by the modern metropolis with its capacity to reduce us all to cogs in a vast machine, faith in the resurrection invites us creatively, lovingly, to weave together bodies of difference, resurrected bodies that belong in the playground of the future, but whose distant laughter comes to us on a warming breeze. To speak of resurrection is to resist death's reductive banality, and this means that the resurrected body cannot be understood simply as some amorphous mass of life. Too often, we are already reduced to that sameness by the vast bureaucracies we inhabit in the modern state. If we are to piece together a vision of life beyond the here and now, we need to find words that express the particularity of each and every life, that lift the person out of the disintegration of death, and carefully shape a future world in which he or she remains loved, recognized and known even if only to God.

The language of life

In a lyrical reflection on the Annunciation, Irigaray says of Mary:

He returns in an unexpected place and in an unexpected guise. In the womb of a woman. Is she the only one left who still has some understanding of the divine? Who still listens silently and gives new flesh to what she perceived in those messages that other people cannot perceive? Can she alone feel the music of the air trembling between the wings of the angels, and make or remake a body from it?[7]

Irigaray suggests that language is the womb in which the body must once more be birthed. In our ways of speaking, in our forms of reasoning, we have forgotten about the body's presence and its participation in the making of culture. When we speak about resurrection, we anticipate a world in which the body must of necessity be a poem, a work of art, a creation of language. We stand before the shadow on the pavement of Hiroshima, the skeleton in the catacombs, the dead tramp in a doorway, the emaciated victim of AIDS, the lonely corpse in a geriatric ward, and, with infinite tenderness and care, we weave a new body of hope for the person that was, is and will be. 'I believe in the resurrection of the dead and the life of the world to come.'

In the film *Schindler's List* there is a moment when we are confronted with the bleached grey misery of death in the camps, when suddenly we see a small red coat, a little girl whom we saw earlier clutching her mother's hand. Out of all the nameless, faceless corpses, she becomes a symbol whose individuality and innocence asserts itself on behalf of every other person there.

Etty Hillesum, a secular Dutch Jew who died in Auschwitz in 1943, recognized the need to preserve a memory of the uniqueness and diversity of peoples, as a way of taking a stand against death and the destruction of memories. She writes, 'The outside world probably thinks of us as a gray, uniform, suffering mass of Jews, and knows nothing of the gulfs and abysses and subtle differences that exist between us. They could never hope to understand.'[8]

In loving protest against this grey uniformity, Hillesum pieces together a tender and tragic tapestry of the camps in which there is 'Life in all its thousands of nuances.'[9] She describes the task she set herself in the transit camp of Westerbok, where against the 'hell' of the transportations she set out to 'write stories about these times that will be like faint brush strokes against the great wordless background of God, Life, Death, Suffering, and Eternity'.[10]

> How can I draw this small village of barracks between heath and sky with a few rapid, delicate, and yet powerful, strokes of the pen? And how can I let others see the many inmates, who have to be deciphered like hieroglyphs, stroke by stroke, until they finally form one great readable and comprehensible whole? One thing I now know for certain: I shall never be able to put down in writing what life itself has spelled out for me in living letters.[11]

Hillesum's words suggest both the imperative and the impossibility of resurrecting the body in language, of letting the individual live on as a faint brush stroke against the 'great wordless background' of mystery.

Practising for eternity

Christian belief in the resurrection of the body has also always entailed disciplining the body and limiting its capacity to make insatiable demands upon us. The body has to be trained for eternity. It has to be firmly taught how to participate in the spirit's freedom and joy, for surrendered to its own devices it is a trap of frustrated and destructive desires and appetites. Catherine of Genoa held an imaginary conversation between the soul, the body and self-love, in which the body and self-love militate against the soul's desires. The soul makes a pact with the body – that they will have alternate weeks in which to satisfy their wishes – but then in exasperation the soul declares:

Of what use is my week to me when you so insist on your needs
that there is no room for mine?
When it is your turn you want your week free and clear;
but when my turn comes up,
you find a thousand things to object to.[12]

But even as she asserts her authority over the body, the soul also insists that her desire is to provide for the body's 'just needs' and 'to lead you to the greatest joy in life'.[13]

Christian asceticism is not popular today. It is no longer thought desirable to fast for Lent as a form of self-discipline and solidarity with the poor, although the fashion and diet industries persuade us that nothing is more noble than to starve the body for vanity. The deferral of pleasure, the practice of self-denial, the value of abstinence, these are regarded as part of a deluded and life-denying religious tradition from which secularism has set us free.

Joan Smith's recent book, *Moralities*, celebrates the 'new *Zeit-geist*'[14] in which humanist beliefs have freed us 'from centuries of bigotry and orthodoxy imposed from above.... In the new scale of values, an absence of transparency and misuse of power are more serious matters than consensual sexual acts between adults.'[15] Smith consistently opposes a public value system based on human rights and equality, to a private sexual sphere devoid of moral significance. But this kind of thinking denies the intricacy of human relationships, where our private domestic and sexual arrangements cannot help but impact on the public realm in subtle but far-reaching ways. Whether we are speaking about the body politic or the sexual body, we need to recognize with Catherine of Genoa that the body has just needs and unjust demands. The liberal Western insistence on every form of physical gratification, including the 'right' to lifelong sexual gratification with as many partners as one chooses, is in itself the substratum upon which the global economy rests. The 'new *Zeitgeist*' of the educated, Western middle classes creates the demand for more and more of everything – commodities, holidays, sexual partners, houses, entertainment – which is paid for in economic exploitation, the tourist industry, the sex trade, the acquisition of property and land from the poor, and the distortion and misrepresentation of human life by the media and the entertainment industry. The liberal separation between the private and the public conceals the fact that it is the private demands of each and every Western citizen, multiplied and magnified many times over, which are destroying the public sphere of the modern world.

The insatiable desires and yearnings that sustain consumerism thrive in the space of hopelessness. The perfect body, the perfect home, the perfect meal, the perfect orgasm, the perfect holiday – all of these are legitimate visions, which become the tormented ambitions of a body trapped in its own mortality. We confuse promise with reality, heaven with earth, eternity with finitude, and we expect to have here and now what is in reality unattainable in this life. The perfect body is the resurrected body in glory. The perfect home is the heavenly city. The perfect meal is the wedding feast when humankind sits down at God's table. The perfect orgasm is the ultimate consummation of our union with God. The perfect holiday is an eternity of praise and rest with God. Understood from this perspective, every human experience can be an epiphany, a fleeting moment of transcendence when we are given a momentary insight into the joy to come. But without that transcendent perspective, the moment's joy becomes a betrayal, because when it goes it leaves only regret and disappointment in its transience, its fragility, its futility.

Resurrection and justice

Resurrection calls us to justice, because it reminds us that everything that earns us envy and respect in this life – not only our material possessions but even our moral virtues and accomplishments – might become the basis of our judgement in the next. The resurrection is an anticipation of the most radical and absolute equality. Flannery O'Connor's short story 'Revelation' tells of a bigoted white woman in the American Deep South, Mrs Turpin, whose self-respect is based on the most carefully articulated social hierarchies in which she gains some superiority because she is neither a 'nigger' nor 'white trash'. The 'revelation' that renders this woman dumbstruck is a vision of the inverse social order of the procession into heaven:

> A visionary light settled in her eyes. She saw the streak as a vast swinging bridge extending upward from the earth through a field of living fire. Upon it a vast horde of souls were rumbling toward heaven. There were whole companies of white-trash, clean for the first time in their lives, and bands of black niggers in white robes, and battalions of freaks and lunatics shouting and clapping and leaping like frogs. And bringing up the end of the procession was a tribe of people whom she recognized at once as those who, like herself and Claud, had always had a little of everything and the God-given wit to use it right. She leaned forward to observe them closer. They were marching behind the others with great

dignity, accountable as they had always been for good order and common sense and respectable behavior. They alone were on key. Yet she could see by their shocked and altered faces that even their virtues were being burned away.[16]

What might we become on that mysterious day when even our virtues are burned away, when the first are last and the last are first, when the poor are filled with good things and the rich sent empty away? Who then will inherit God's kingdom, and who will turn away in wounded pride, deciding perhaps with Milton's Satan that, after a lifetime of self-aggrandizement and satisfied ambition, it is 'Better to reign in Hell, than serve in Heav'n'?

Of course, we might readily acknowledge that, like O'Connor's Mrs Turpin, we are prey to every kind of arrogance and condescension, but the saints warn us that we are most vulnerable when we believe that we have won this struggle. There is a saying, 'I used to be conceited, but now I'm perfect.' How often do Christians fall into that deadly destructive lie of their own perfection? In Teresa of Avila's *Interior Castle*, spiritual pride is a particularly dangerous stage in the contemplative life, a stage when the morally upright and virtuous person becomes certain of his or her righteousness in the eyes of God and refuses any form of correction or criticism. In Matthew 25, we are told that we will be judged by our care for the poor, prisoners, the naked, the destitute, not by the intensity of our faith. The righteous appear not even to recognize Christ in their care for the poor, while the sinners are those who cry 'Lord, Lord' while turning their backs on those in need. In the end, we are judged not for our piety nor even for our faith, but for our love of our neighbour in need.

Thérèse of Lisieux spent her short life determined to become a saint, but her *Story of a Soul* is as much about the loss of faith as about faith itself. She came to the recognition that it was love, not faith, that was the greatest affirmation of God, and she was able to face even the prospect of her own annihilation with a candour that the great nihilist, Nietzsche, might have identified with. She writes that

the voice of unbelievers came to mock me out of the darkness: 'You dream of light, of a fragrant land, you dream that their Creator will be yours for ever and you think you will one day leave behind this fog in which you languish. Hope on! Hope on! And look forward to death! But it will give you, not what you hope for, but a still darker night, the night of annihilation.'[17]

It is this experience that enables her to recognize that 'in order for love to be fully satisfied it must descend to nothingness and transform that nothingness to living fire'.[18] For all her cloying sentimentality, perhaps the honesty of Thérèse's vision of love's little way has much to teach us.

To speak of the resurrection of the body, we must speak as love's protest against nothingness. In a world surrendered to extremes of despair, the language of hope becomes the language of love, and it is love that makes resurrection present among us. Love reclaims the body from its disintegration into chaos and destruction, and pieces it together bone by bone and memory by memory. The greater the disintegration, the more awesome is love's redeeming power.

Love and hope are not the same thing, but perhaps they are inseparable. Hope is love's commitment to the future as well as love's memory of the past. It is the connecting thread we weave into the fabric of history. It is fragile, almost invisible against the canvas of time. It is by its very nature particular, attentive and quiet. When it shouts its message and declares its presence too loudly, it becomes an ideology or a Utopian fantasy. Hope is something subtle, perhaps not even recognizable. It refuses to yield to despair but offers no platitude, no false word of comfort, no response other than its own elusive presence. And sometimes it must declare its presence not even as a future eventuality but as love here and now, before and beyond the terror of death.

Redemption

I want to end this reflection on resurrection by returning to that vision of Christ rising from hell. This time, it is the backdrop not to the dancing bodies of women but to the heartache of women who are shaping a body of love in the very depths of hell. The following two extracts are taken from interviews with widows of men who died in Chernobyl, speaking to the Russian journalist Svetlana Alexievich. Some might say that these voices belong in the chapter on death, not in this chapter on resurrection, but that is not so. They belong here because they are voices of mystery, love's mystery, which the grave cannot contain. In the most intimate and tender language, these two wives lift the beloved bodies of their men out of death's grip and caress them into eternity, an eternity of an unthinkable present and an unimaginable future, finely woven out of the most delicate of words.

Ludmila Ignatenko, wife of the deceased firefighter Vasily Ignatenko:

> I don't know what to tell you about. Death or love? Or is it one and the same? What shall I tell you? We were newly-weds.... In the middle of the night, I heard a noise. I looked out the window. He saw me and said, 'Shut the windows and get back to sleep. There's a fire at the reactor. I'll be back soon.' ... They had gone off to the fire without their protective gear, just in their shirt sleeves. They had not been warned, they had been summoned as if to a normal fire....

Sometimes I hear his voice. Alive. Even photographs don't have the same effect on me as the voice. But he never calls me, not even in my dreams. It's I who call him.... I knew that I had to hide my pregnancy. Otherwise they wouldn't let me see him.... The whole world had narrowed to a single point for me....

He began changing – every day I found a new man. The burns were surfacing. In his mouth, his tongue, his cheeks – first they were small ulcers and then they spread. The mucous membranes came off in layers. In white sheets. The colour of his face. The colour of his body. Blue. Red. Greyish brown. And it was mine, I loved every inch of it. I can't say it! You can't write it!...

I remember a piece of conversation. In my memory. Someone telling me, 'You must not forget: what you have here is no longer your husband, the man you love, but a radioactive object with a high density of contamination. You are not a suicide case. Get a grip on yourself.' And me, like a crazy woman, 'I love him! I love him!' ... The nurses let me in. At first they tried to talk me out of it. 'You're young. What are you doing? He's no longer human, he's a reactor. You'll both burn to death.'...

The last two days at the hospital, I would lift his arm, and the bone would rattle loose, the flesh had separated from it. He coughed up pieces of lung and liver. He was choking on his insides. I would wrap bandages around my hand and scoop it all out of his mouth. It's impossible to tell this! It shouldn't be written! It's all so private. So loved....

I dream. He and I are walking on water....

All the people from the station live around me, the people we call the watchers. They had worked at the reactor all their lives.... They are dying, but no one has questioned them, really. About what we've lived through. No one wants to hear about death. About the horror. But I have told you about love. About how I loved.[19]

Ludmila gave birth to a baby daughter, Natashenka, two months after Vasily's death. The baby lived for four hours. Because of the radiation, she had cirrhosis of the liver and congenital heart defects.

Valentina Timofeyevna Panasevich, wife of a clean-up crew member:

I was so happy when he came back. We made it a holiday at home, as we always did for his return. I have this very long and very beautiful nightgown. I wore it. I love expensive lingerie, all my stuff is good, but this gown is special. Festive. For our first night. I know his body by heart, I've kissed it all.... His lymph nodes were swollen when he came back. I felt them with my lips....

Love! it wasn't even love, it was a long falling in love. I used to dance in front of the mirror in the mornings; I'm beautiful, I'm young, he loves me! Now I have trouble remembering my face, the face I had when I was with him. I don't see that face in the mirror any more....

'Oh, more blood.' I would scream. From his neck, his cheeks, his ears. In all directions. I would bring cold water and make compresses – but they didn't help. It was horrible. The whole pillow would be covered with blood. I'd put a basin under the bleeding. The streams would strike it like milk hitting a bucket. That sound – so peaceful and countrylike. I can hear it at night even now.... There are private things. I was sitting next to him. He was asleep. He had such beautiful hair. I cut off a lock. He opened his eyes, saw what I had in my hands, and smiled....

We brought back the urn. I wasn't afraid, I felt inside and there was something small, like shells at the beach, in the sand. Those were his hip bones....

How will I go on living? I haven't told you everything. Not everything. I was happy. I loved him madly. Maybe you shouldn't use my name. There are secrets. People say prayers in private. Whispering. [*Pause.*] No, use my name. Say it to God. I want to understand. I also want to understand why we are given suffering? What is it for? At first I thought that, after all that, some dark look would appear in my eyes, something alien. What has saved me? What has pushed me towards life? Brought me back? My son. I still have a son, our son together. He's been sick a long time. He's grown up but he sees the world through a child's eyes. The eyes of a five-year-old....

We'll wait together. I will whisper my Chernobyl prayer. He sees the world through a child's eyes.[20]

And so we come to this point in our history, this melting point. What has saved us? Why do we not all have that dark and alien look in our eyes, when we have gazed upon such monstrous truths?

Svetlana Alexievich explains her motivation for writing the book. She wanted to write about 'missed history', not about the events but about 'the feelings, the sensations of people who had touched the unknown. The mystery.' She goes on:

Chernobyl is a mystery that we have to solve. Perhaps that is a task for the twenty-first century. A challenge. What has humanity discovered and guessed about itself? In its attitude towards the world? A reconstruction of feelings, not of events.... More than once, I had the feeling that I was recording the future.[21]

'A reconstruction of feelings'

Somewhere in our long and tangled history, we became preoccupied with events, with facts, with science. Now we face the challenge of the future, and perhaps only a reconstruction of feelings will help us to move beyond the death of science, the death that science so often delivers in its promise of life. 'I hate your science! I hate it!' screamed Ludmila when her baby daughter died.

But we cannot go back before nor forward beyond science. We cannot not know. That is why the acquisition of knowledge is always a loss of innocence, a fall from grace. According to Thomas Aquinas, the beatitude of mourning 'is the special beatitude for those whose calling it is to extend the boundaries of knowledge'.[22] As human beings we will continue to discover, to explore, to fail, to destroy, and to hope. That is Eve's unique and precious legacy to us – the inseparability of knowledge and mourning. But through the reconstruction of feeling, we can suffuse our world with grace again, breathe into it the mysterious life that makes everything gift. These women of Chernobyl know that they are trying to say what cannot be said. 'I keep saying the wrong things to you. Not the words I want.' 'I don't know if one can talk about this? In so many words.'

Words. Images. Music. Art. The beauty and despair of human existence struggling to rise through silence and express itself, insisting on the power to communicate, to understand, to unravel the mystery, to make meaning, to speak life's presence in the midst of the dead. In the Chernobyl interviews, a man who wants to be named only as 'Nikolai, servant of the Lord', muses aloud:

A question: is the world captured in words true? Words stand between man and his soul. It's like that.... Every living thing on four legs looks to the earth, is drawn to the earth. Only man stands on the earth but lifts his hands and head to the sky. Towards prayer, towards God. The old women in church pray, 'God forgive us our sins.' But the scientist, the engineer, the soldier do not admit that. They think, 'I have nothing to repent. Why should I?' It's like that. I pray simply. In my head. Lord, take me! Hear me! Man is sophisticated only in evil. But how simple and accessible he is in plain words of love.[23]

The men of science and war do not repent, but the old women do. The mothers whose children and grandchildren create such destruction and such beauty. Forgive us, for we know not what we do. We must whisper a Chernobyl prayer, and see the world through a child's eyes.

The bride

Fazzini's sculpture suggests love lightly, joyfully rising from the chaos of death. The women of Chernobyl, lovingly tending the dying bodies of their husbands, show us love's power and love's grief. Against the annihilating verdict – 'He's no longer human, he's a reactor' – a wife makes love to her dead husband in words, and she invites us into the mystery of our being – hers, his, yours, mine – a being which will not die as long as love continues to speak of us, for us and with us.

After the concert, we step outside into the warm Roman night. St Peter's is illuminated in soft gold. It looks serene, its ambiguities and offences smudged beneath a benign moon. The city calls, beckons, invites, from all her darkened alleys and brash shop windows, from the roar of her traffic and the voices of her people. Come, taste and see that the Lord is good.

The city. Brave, beautiful, corrupt, polluted. The city moving in the vast shadow of time, with the glow of a thousand Chernobyls around her. The city, beautiful as a bride, coming down out of the heavens to greet her beloved.

'Let's buy some champagne and cake and have a picnic in the park,' he said, glowing. Under the stars! That's what he was like. We sat on a bench in Gorky Park until morning. I've never had a birthday like that in my life and that's when I said, 'Marry me. I love you so much!' ... I was so happy! I wouldn't change a thing in my life, even if someone had warned me from above, from the stars.... I remember the night he died I was beside him. And suddenly there was this bit of smoke. The second time I saw it was at the crematorium. His soul. No one else saw it, but I did. I felt that we had seen each other once again.

(Valentina Timofeyevna Panasevich)

I loved him! I didn't know yet just how much I loved him! We had only recently got married. We'd be walking down the street. He would pick me up and spin me round. And shower me with kisses. People would walk past and smile....

May 9th. Victory Day. He had always told me, 'You can't imagine how beautiful Moscow is! Especially on Victory Day, with the fireworks. I want you to see that.' I was sitting next to him in the ward. He opened his eyes.

'Is it day or night?'

'Nine p.m.'

'Open the window! The fireworks!'

I opened the window. We were on the eighth floor, we could see the whole city below us! A bouquet of fire burst into the sky.

'That's gorgeous!'

'I promised you I would show you Moscow. I promised I would give you flowers on holidays as long as I lived.'

I turned around, and he was getting three carnations from under his pillow. He had paid a nurse to get them.

I ran over and kissed him. 'My darling! My love!'

(Ludmila Ignatenko)

Who is this coming up from the desert
leaning on her Beloved?

I awakened you under the apple tree,
there where your mother conceived you,
there where she who gave birth to you conceived you.
Set me like a seal on your heart,
like a seal on your arm.
For love is strong as Death,
jealousy relentless as Sheol.
The flash of it is a flash of fire,
a flame of Yahweh himself.
Love no flood can quench,
no torrents drown.

(Song of Songs)

Then I saw a new heaven and a new earth; the first heaven and the first earth had disappeared now, and there was no longer any sea. I saw the holy city, and the new Jerusalem, coming down from God out of heaven, as beautiful as a bride all dressed for her husband. Then I heard a loud voice call from the throne, 'You see this city? Here God lives among people. He will make his home among them; they shall be his people, and he will be their God; his name is God-with-them. He will wipe away all tears from their eyes; there will be no more death, and no more mourning or sadness. The world of the past has gone.

(Revelation)

Notes

1. Quoted in Kari Elisabeth Børresen, *Subordination and Equivalence – the Nature and Role of Women in Augustine and Thomas Aquinas*, new edition (Kampen: Kok Pharos Publishing House, 1995), p. 86.

2. William L. Lawrence, *Men and Atoms* (New York: Simon & Schuster, 1959), p. 197, quoted in Daly, *Pure Lust*, p. 126.

3. Grace Jantzen, *Becoming Divine: Towards a Feminist Philosophy of Religion* (Manchester: Manchester University Press, 1998).

4. Takeharu Terao, *A Personal Record of Hiroshima A-bomb Survival* on *http://www.coara.or.jp/~ryoji/abomb/a-bomb1.html*.

5. Valentina Timofeyevna Panasevich, quoted in Svetlana Alexievich, *Voices from Chernobyl: Chronicle of the Future*, trans. Antonina W. Bouis (London: Aurum Press, 1999), p. 193.

6. Camille Paglia, *Sex and Violence, or Nature and Art* (London: Penguin 60s, 1995), p. 55.

7. Luce Irigaray, *Marine Lover of Friedrich Nietzsche*, trans. Gillian C. Gill (New York: Columbia University Press, 1991), pp. 175–6.

8. Hillesum, *An Interrupted Life*, p. 353.

9. Ibid., p. 247.

10. Ibid., p. 172.

11. Ibid., p. 210.

12. Catherine of Genoa, *The Spiritual Dialogue*, in Amy Oden (ed.), *In Her Words: Women's Writings in the History of Christian Thought* (London: SPCK, 1995), pp. 211–12.

13. Ibid., p. 213.

14. Joan Smith, *Moralities: Sex, Money and Power in the Twenty-first Century* (London: Allen Lane, 2001), p. xv.

15. Ibid., p. xi.

16. Flannery O'Connor, *The Complete Stories* (London and Boston, MA: Faber & Faber, 1990), p. 508.

17. Thérèse of Lisieux, *The Story of a Soul*, p. 118.

18. Ibid., p. 155.

19. Alexievich, *Voices from Chernobyl*, pp. 5–18.

20. Ibid., pp. 185–94.

21. Ibid., pp. 19–21.

22. Donald Nichol, *The Beatitude of Truth: Reflections of a Lifetime* (London: Darton, Longman & Todd, 1997), p. 5.

23. In Alexievich, *Voices from Chernobyl*, p. 55.

Bibliography

Alexievich, Svetlana, *Voices from Chernobyl: Chronicle of the Future*, trans. Antonina W. Bouis (London: Aurum Press, 1999)

Anderson, Bonnie S. and Zinsser, Judith P., *A History of their Own: Women in Europe from Prehistory to the Present*, Vol. I (London: Penguin, 1988)

Anselm, *The Prayers and Meditations of Saint Anselm with the Proslogion*, trans. Sister Benedicta Ward, SLG (London: Penguin, 1973)

Aquinas, Thomas, *Summa Theologiae: A Concise Translation*, ed. Timothy McDermott (London: Methuen, 1992)

Ashe, Geoffrey, *The Virgin* (London: Routledge & Kegan Paul, 1976)

Ashley, Kathleen and Sheingorn, Pamela (eds), *Interpreting Cultural Symbols: Saint Anne in Late Medieval Society* (Athens GA and London: University of Georgia Press, 1997)

Augustine of Hippo, *Concerning the City of God against the Pagans*, ed. David Knowles, trans. Henry Bettenson (London: Penguin, 1981)

Aulén, Gustav, *Christus Victor: An Historical Study of the Three Main Types of the Idea of the Atonement*, trans. A. G. Herbert (London: SPCK, 1961)

Baring, Anne and Cashford, Jules, *The Myth of the Goddess: Evolution of an Image* (London: Arkana, Penguin, 1993)

Beattie, Tina, *God's Mother, Eve's Advocate* (London: Continuum, 2002)

Benko, Stephen, *The Virgin Goddess: Studies in the Pagan and Christian Roots of Mariology* (New York: E. J. Brill, 1993)

Børresen, Kari Elisabeth, *Subordination and Equivalence – The Nature and*

Role of Women in Augustine and Thomas Aquinas, (Kampen: Kok Pharos Publishing House, 1995)

Boss, Sarah Jane, *Empress and Handmaid: On Nature and Gender in the Cult of the Virgin Mary* (London and New York: Cassell, 2000)

Brandenbarg, Tom, 'St Anne and her Family', in Lène Dresen-Coenders (ed.), *Saints and She-Devils: Images of Women in the Fifteenth and Sixteenth Centuries* (London: Rubicon Press, 1987)

Brown, Peter, *The Cult of the Saints: Its Rise and Function in Latin Christianity* (Chicago, IL: University of Chicago Press, 1981)

Buby, Bertrand, SM, *Mary of Galilee, Volume III, The Marian Heritage of the Early Church* (New York: Alba House, St Pauls, 1997)

Bynum, Caroline Walker, *Fragmentation and Redemption: Essays on Gender and the Human Body in Medieval Religion* (New York: Zone Books, 1994)

Catherine of Siena, *The Dialogue*, translated with an introduction by Suzanne Noffke O.P., preface by Giuliana Cavallini (Mahwah NJ: Paulist Press, 1980)

Chodorow, Nancy, *The Reproduction of Mothering: Psychoanalysis and the Sociology of Gender* (Berkeley, CA: University of California Press, 1978)

Clark, Kenneth, *The Nude: A Study in Ideal Art* (London: John Murray, 1956)

Crace, Jim, *Being Dead* (London: Penguin, 2000)

Daly, Mary, *Pure Lust: Elemental Feminist Philosophy* (London: The Women's Press, 1984)

——, *The Church and the Second Sex* (Boston, MA: Beacon Press, 1985)

de Beauvoir, Simone, *The Second Sex*, trans. H. M. Parshley (London: Penguin, 1972)

della Portella, Ivana, *Subterranean Rome*, photos by Mark E. Smith (Rome: Konemann, 1999)

Dogmatic Canons and Decrees of the Council of Trent and Vatican Council I plus the Decree on the Immaculate Conception and the Syllabus of Errors of Pope Pius IX (Rockford, IL: Tan Books, 1977)

Elshtain, Jean Bethke, 'The Power and Powerlessness of Women', in

Gisela Bock and Susan James (eds), *Beyond Equality and Difference: Citizenship, Feminist Politics and Female Subjectivity* (London and New York: Routledge, 1992)

——, *Public Man, Private Woman: Women in Social and Political Thought* (Princeton, NJ: Princeton University Press, 1993)

Ferguson, John, *War and Peace in the World's Religions* (London: Sheldon Press, 1977)

Fiorenza, Elisabeth Schüssler, *In Memory of Her: A Feminist Theological Reconstruction of Christian Origins*, 2nd edn (London: SCM Press, 1995)

Firmicus Maternicus, *The Error of the Pagan Religions*, trans. and annotated by Clarence A. Forbes (New York and Ramsey, NJ: Newman Press, 1970)

Fitzgerald, Constance, OCD, 'Impasse and Dark Night', in Joann Wolski Conn (ed.), *Women's Spirituality: Resources for Christian Development* (Mahwah, NJ: Paulist Press, 1986)

Flannery, Austin, OP (ed.), *Vatican Collection: Vatican Council II, Volume 1, The Conciliar and Postconciliar Documents* (Dublin: Dominican Publications; New Town, NSW: E. J. Dwyer, 1992)

Foucault, Michel, *The History of Sexuality, Volume 1 – An Introduction* (London: Penguin, 1990)

Fox, Robin Lane, *Pagans and Christians in the Mediterranean World from the Second Century AD to the Conversion of Constantine* (London: Viking Penguin, 1986)

Freud, Sigmund, *The Origins of Religion*, trans. James Strachey, ed. Albert Dickson, The Penguin Freud Library, Vol. 13 (London: Penguin, 1990)

——, *Civilization, Society and Religion*, trans. James Strachey, ed. Albert Dickson, The Penguin Freud Library, Vol. 12 (London: Penguin, 1991)

Frymer-Kensky, Tikva, *In the Wake of the Goddesses: Women, Culture and the Biblical Transformation of Pagan Myth* (New York: Fawcett Columbine, 1992)

Gebara, Ivone, 'The Face of Transcendence as a Challenge to the Reading of the Bible in Latin America', in Elisabeth Schüssler

Fiorenza (ed.), *Searching the Scriptures: A Feminist Introduction* (London: SCM Press, 1993)

George, Timothy, 'A Radically Christian Witness for Peace', in Haim Gordon and Leonard Grob (eds), *Education for Peace: Testimonies from World Religions* (Maryknoll, NY: Orbis, 1987)

Gilligan, Carol, *In a Different Voice: Psychological Theory and Women's Development* (Cambridge, MA, and London: Harvard University Press, 1993)

Girard, René, *Violence and the Sacred*, trans. Patrick Gregory (Baltimore, MD: Johns Hopkins University Press, 1977)

——, *Things Hidden Since the Foundation of the World*, trans. Stephen Bann and Michael Metteer (London: The Athlone Press, 1987)

——, *The Girard Reader*, ed. James G. Williams (New York: Crossroad Herder, 1996)

Graef, Hilda, *Mary: A History of Doctrine and Devotion*, combined edn (London: Sheed & Ward, 1994)

Green, Dave, 'From Tree to Rhizome: Pagan Spirituality, Science and Resistance in the New Millenium', in Ursula King (ed.), *Spirituality and Society in the New Millennium* (Brighton: Sussex Academic Press, 2001)

Guinness, Michele, *Tapestry of Voices: Meditations on Women's Lives* (London: Triangle, 1996)

Gutiérrez, Gustavo, *A Theology of Liberation: History, Politics, and Salvation* (London: SCM Press, 1988)

Herlihy, David, 'The Family and Religious Ideology in Medieval Europe', in D. Herlihy and A. Molho (eds), *Women, Family and Society in Medieval Europe* (New York and Oxford: Berghahn Books, 1995)

Hildegard of Bingen: An Anthology, eds Fiona Bowie and Oliver Davies (London: SPCK, 1992)

Hillesum, Etty, *An Interrupted Life: The Diaries, 1941–1943 and Letters from Westerbork*, trans. Arnold J. Pomerans (New York: Henry Holt, 1996)

Hughes, Gerard W., *God of Surprises* (London: Darton, Longman & Todd, 1987)

Irigaray, Luce, *This Sex Which is Not One*, trans. Catherine Porter with Carolyn Burke (Ithaca, NY: Cornell University Press, 1985)

——, *Marine Lover of Friedrich Nietzsche*, trans. Gillian C. Gill (New York: Columbia University Press, 1991)

——, *je, tu, nous: Toward a Culture of Difference*, trans. Alison Martin (New York and London: Routledge, 1993)

——, *Thinking the Difference*, trans. Karen Montin (London: The Athlone Press, 1994)

Jantzen, Grace, *Becoming Divine: Towards a Feminist Philosophy of Religion* (Manchester: Manchester University Press, 1998)

Jay, Nancy, 'Sacrifice as Remedy for Having Been Born of Woman', in Clarissa W. Atkinson, Constance H. Buchanan, and Margaret R. Miles (eds), *Immaculate and Powerful: The Female in Sacred Image and Social Reality* (Boston, MA: Crucible, 1987)

Jensen, Anne, *God's Self-Confident Daughters: Early Christianity and the Liberation of Women*, trans. O. C. Dean Jr (Louisville, KY: Westminster John Knox Press, 1996)

John Paul II, *Original Unity of Man and Woman – Catechesis on the Book of Genesis* (Boston, MA: St Paul Books and Media, 1981)

——, *Mulieris Dignitatem: Apostolic Letter on the Dignity and Vocation of Women on the Occasion of the Marin Year* (London: Catholic Truth Society, 1988)

——, *Crossing the Threshold of Hope*, ed. Vittorio Messori, trans. Jenny and Martha McPhee (London: Jonathan Cape, 1994)

——, *Evangelium Vitae: Encyclical Letter on the Value and Inviolability of Human Life* (London: Catholic Truth Society, 1995)

Jonas, Hans, 'The Right to Die' in Thomas A. Shannon (ed.), *Bioethics*, 3rd edn (Mahwah, NJ: St Pauls, 1997), pp. 195–208

Julian of Norwich, *The Revelation of Divine Love*, trans. M.-L. del Mastro (Tunbridge Wells: Burns & Oates, 1994)

King, Ursula, *Women and Spirituality* (Basingstoke: Macmillan, 1990)

Kovachevski, Christo, *The Madonna in Western Painting*, trans. Nikola Georgiev (London: Cromwell Editions, 1991)

Kristeva, Julia, *Powers of Horror – An Essay on Abjection*, trans. Leon S. Roudiez (New York: Columbia University Press, 1982)

——, *Tales of Love*, trans. Leon S. Roudiez (New York: Columbia University Press, 1987)

Lerner, Gerda, *The Creation of Feminist Consciousness: From the Middle Ages to Eighteen-seventy* (Oxford and New York: Oxford University Press, 1993)

Livius, Thomas, *The Blessed Virgin in the Fathers of the First Six Centuries* (London: Burns & Oates; New York: Benziger Brothers, 1893)

MacCulloch, Diarmaid, *Groundwork of Christian History* (London: Epworth Press, 1987)

Magonet, Jonathan, *A Rabbi's Bible* (London: SCM Press, 1991)

Matthews, Melvyn, *Both Alike to Thee: The Retrieval of the Mystical Way* (London: SPCK, 2000)

Merchant, Carolyn, *The Death of Nature: Women, Ecology and the Scientific Revolution* (San Francisco, CA: Harper & Row, 1979)

Meynell, Alice, *Mary, the Mother of Jesus* (London: The Medici Society, 1923)

Midgeley, Mary, *Wickedness: A Philosophical Essay* (London and New York: Ark Paperbacks, 1986)

Miles, Margaret, *Carnal Knowing: Female Nakedness and Religious Meaning in the Christian West* (Tunbridge Wells: Burns & Oates, 1992)

Mitchell, Juliet and Rose, Jacqueline (eds), *Feminine Sexuality: Jacques Lacan and the Ecole Freudienne*, trans. Jacqueline Rose (Basingstoke: Macmillan, 1982)

Moltmann, Jürgen, 'The Inviting Unity of the Triune God', in Claude Geffré and Jean Pièrre Jossua (eds), *Monotheism, Concilium 177* (Edinburgh: T. & T. Clark, 1985)

Moreno, Paolo and Stefani, Chiara, *The Borghese Gallery* (Milan: Touring Club Italiano, 2000)

Neuberger, Julia (ed.), *The Things that Matter: An Anthology of Women's Spiritual Poetry* (London: Kyle Cathie, 1992)

Nichol, Donald, *The Beatitude of Truth: Reflections of a Lifetime* (London: Darton, Longman & Todd, 1997)

O'Connor, Flannery, *The Complete Stories* (London and Boston, MA: Faber & Faber, 1990)

Oden, Amy (ed.), *In Her Words: Women's Writings in the History of Christian Thought* (London: SPCK, 1995)

O'Donoghue, Noel Dermot, *Heaven in Ordinarie: Prayer as Transcendence* (Edinburgh: T. & T. Clark, 1996)

Owen, Richard, 'Art Lovers Practise the Art of Love', in *The Times*, 11 June 2001

Pagels, Elaine, *Adam, Eve and the Serpent* (London: Weidenfeld & Nicolson, 1988)

Paglia, Camille, *Sex and Violence, or Nature and Art* (London: Penguin 60s, 1995)

Pearson, John, *Arena: The Story of the Colosseum* (London: Thames and Hudson, 1973)

Perry, Nicholas and Echeverría, Loreto, *Under the Heel of Mary* (London: Routledge, 1988)

Pustka, Josef, *The Basilica of Santa Maria Maggiore* (Rome: D.EDI.T.s.r.l., 1997)

Ruether, Rosemary Radford, *Sexism and God-Talk* (London: SCM Press, 1992)

Ruston, Roger, *War of Religions, Religion of War* (Manchester: Blackfriars Publications, 1993)

Smith, Joan, *Moralities: Sex, Money and Power in the Twenty-first Century* (London: Allen Lane, 2001)

Sobrino, Jon, *Jesus the Liberator*, trans. Paul Burns and Francis McDonagh (Tunbridge Wells: Burns & Oates, 1994)

Stevenson, J., *A New Eusebius: Documents Illustrating the History of the Church to AD 337*, new edn, rev. W. H. C. Frend (London: SPCK, 1987)

Stuart, Elizabeth, *Spitting at Dragons: Towards a Feminist Theology of Sainthood* (London: Mowbrays, 1996)

Takeharu Terao, *A Personal Record of Hiroshima A-bomb Survival* on *www.coara.or.jp/~ryoji/abomb/a-bomb1.html*

Thérèse of Lisieux, *The Autobiography of Saint Thérèse of Lisieux: The Story of a Soul*, trans. John Beevers (New York: Doubleday, 1989)

Trible, Phyllis, *God and the Rhetoric of Sexuality* (Philadelphia, OH: Fortress Press, 1978)

Turner, Victor, *Dramas, Fields, and Metaphors: Symbolic Action in Human Society* (Ithaca, NY, and London: Cornell University Press, 1974)

Venturi, Adolfo, *The Madonna: A Pictorial Representation of the Life and Death of the Mother of Our Lord Jesus Christ by the Painters and Sculptors of Christendom in more than 500 of their Works*, trans. Alice Meynell (London: Burns & Oates, n.d.)

Vicinus, Martha, *Independent Women: Work and Community for Single Women, 1850–1920* (Chicago, IL: University of Chicago Press, 1988)

Vickers, Jeanne, *Women and War* (London and New Jersey: Zed Books, 1993)

Warner, Marina, *Alone of All her Sex: the Myth and the Cult of the Virgin Mary* (London: Picador, 1990)

Website of Borgehese Gallery *www.galleriaborghese.it/default-en.htm*

Website of the Roman Curia *http://www.vatican.va/roman_curia/congregations/ccdds/documents/*

Weidemann, Thomas, 'Emperors, Gladiators and Christians', in *Omnibus*, 22 (September 1991), pp. 26–8

White, Lynn, Jr, 'The Historical Roots of our Ecological Crisis', in Mary Heather MacKinnon and Moni McIntyre (eds), *Readings in Ecology and Feminist Theology* (Kansas City, KS: Sheed & Ward, 1995)

Winnicott, D. W., *Playing and Reality* (London: Tavistock, 1971)

——, *Human Nature* (London: Free Association Books, 1991)

DATE DUE